Cauld Blasts
and
Clishmaclavers

Cauld Blasts
and
Clishmaclavers

A treasury of
1,000 Scottish words

Robin A. Crawford

Elliott&Thompson

First published 2020 by
Elliott and Thompson Limited
2 John Street
London WC1N 2ES
www.eandtbooks.com

ISBN: 978-1-78396-478-9

INTRODUCTION

They speak in riddles north beyond the Tweed,
The plain, pure English they can deftly read;
Yet when without the book they come to speak,
Their lingo seems half English and half Greek.

... This room they call the **but** and that the ben,
And what they do not know they **dinna ken**.
On keen cold days they say the wind **blaws snell**,
And they have words that Johnson could not spell,
And when they wipe their nose they **dicht** their **byke**,
As **imph'm** which means – anything you like;
While some, though purely English, and well known,
Have yet a Scottish meaning of their own:

... To **crack** is to converse; the **lift**'s the sky;
And **bairns** are said to **greet** when children cry.

Robert Leighton, 'Scotch Words', 1869

The 2011 Scottish Census found that more than 150 languages other than English are used in Scottish homes.

Scotland is a nation of peoples woven together like a **tartan** or **tweed**. The overall effect may be one of **Scottishness** but the individual threads have a uniqueness of their own. Celt and Pict; Gael and Angle; Norse and Norman; Roman and Romany; Italian, English and Irish; African, American, Asian and Australasian and many more have all brought something to the lexicographers' **ceilidh** that is our language – and continue to do so.

At the re-convening of the Scottish parliament in July 2016 the poem 'Threshold' by the Scots **Makar** Jackie Kay was read. In it Kay beseeches the parliament, the nation, not to ca' **canny** but to be bold and open our hearts and to welcome the future with the voices of all the peoples who call Scotland **hame**. She uses Scots to call out a welcome not only to share our domestic living space but also to repopulate the wide open spaces of Scotland, historically emptied of people, and to create a brilliant **gathering of the clans** of the world.

Poetry is by its very essence a celebration of the diversity and meanings of language used to describe the human condition and the world around us. It has long been a **kist** of riches for the **Scots** tongue. It is from the works of Kay's predecessors as **makars** that many of the words we use today have been preserved – in the poetry of Henryson and Dunbar, Ramsay and Fergusson, Scott and Stevenson, MacDiarmid and Jacob, Lochhead and MacCaig – but most of all in the words of Robert Burns. It is through Burns that many Scots kept Scotland in their hearts as well as on their tongues whether they were in domestic service in London, digging railroads in America, running tea plantations in India, whaling in the Davis Strait, herding sheep in the Australian outback or in the rain-sodden trenches of Flanders.

At the end of his long life my great-great-great-grandfather published a pamphlet in praise of Robert Burns. In it he wrote:

> I have been an enthusiastic admirer of Robert Burns and his
> works, ever since I was first able to read them. In July 1806
> I went from Forfarshire to Dumfries, to see the spot where his
> remains were interred. I found his grave covered with a plain
> slab, and literally obeyed the Poet's request – drew near
> And o'er this grassy heap sang dool
> And dropped a tear.

Two centuries later, Burns' work continues to speak to people. His poems, songs and language contain an immutable Scottishness that touches my soul like no other; my wife and I had his words read at our wedding. He is quoted more than any other writer in this book.

Burns' language grew from the Ayrshire land his family farmed but he was also well read and well travelled; in Edinburgh he moved within

Enlightenment circles, and he corresponded far and wide. From all over the country he harvested words, poems and stories, ploughing them back into his verse. And he was not just a poet but a collector and re-worker of traditional songs, which had been passed down orally through generations; he contributed them to that great compendium of song *The Scots Musical Museum*. He showed an awareness of a unique language that was under threat and needed to be preserved.

Scots is perhaps best described as a *Halbsprache* – a half-language – and has been developing since the start of the second millennium. Its roots are Germanic with many similarities to Middle English but with a history all its own.

Historians and lexicographers call the language of the early period from about 1100 to 1700 'Older Scots' and use 'Modern Scots' for the period from 1700 to the present. Sometimes the term 'Middle Scots' is used to describe the language from 1450 to 1700. It was during this period that Scots came under pressure as never before from a unique combination of technological advancement, religious dissent and high international politics – French and English influences at court waxed and waned as the two powerful kingdoms sought influence and control over Scotland.

The eventual Union of the Crowns of Scotland with England in 1603 saw the royal court – once the home of poet prince King James I (1394–1437), of Robert Henryson (*c.* 1460–1505) and William Dunbar (1459–*c.* 1530) – move to London, and with the Union of the Parliaments in 1707 the legislature joined it. While Scots language remained unique in law, education and religion, it lost the authority of being the language of power and governance.

Even in the surviving centres of influence, the creeping Anglicisation over Old Scots came, driven by the printing press rather than by high politics. Although Chepman and Myllar were printing in Edinburgh by 1508, the printing industry in England was more prolific and thus more affordable. Literature, especially 'high' literature, was more likely to be printed in English and Latin than in Scots, including bibles and tracts spreading the word of the Reformation. Even the *King James Bible* is in English despite being commissioned by the Scottish monarch.

Both sides of James VI's earthly administration used English and throughout the seventeenth century it became the dominant language of government as well. In the ruling classes of both kingdoms, aristocratic intermarriage cemented English as the language of power and Scots came to be regarded as provincial, outdated and even seditious. Ever since, Scots has been seen as the language of the 'common people', printed in chapbook, pamphlet and ballad; spoken on the farm, the bar or the **scheme**. There are many examples to be found in the book.

Even before Burns, poets had been aware of this decline of the language of their forbearers and had sought to preserve it. Earlier in the eighteenth century, for example, Allan Ramsay wrote his libretto for *The Gentle Shepherd*, Scotland's first opera, set in the pastoral Pentland Hills, while Robert Fergusson's poetry portrayed urban Edinburgh life. They understood Scots held within it not just the voice of Scotland but its very character. Through the use of vernacular Scots, poets and writers captured and nurtured a language in decline, while also popularising it and spreading its readership. The Romantic sentiment of the late eighteenth and early nineteenth centuries adored the Scots of Scott and the **Scottishness** of Byron and while that might have led to the **tartanry** of King George IV and **Balmorality** of Queen Victoria, it certainly boosted the interest in the country's history and the remnants of that past, including its language.

In addition, an increasingly large number of exiled Scots, whether in the ever expanding urbanised centres or in far-off imperial outposts, were nostalgic for their homeland. In its language they found an easily transportable memento of home: the song sung to the rhythm of a pickaxe's swinging; the small **quair** of poems that fitted in an apron pocket; the **cornkister** at a tropical **ceilidh**.

This Scots, though, is the language of poetry chosen for the sound and texture it added to the verse and not necessarily the living language of every day. As the nineteenth century progressed, upper- and middle-class Scotland looked fondly on the traditional and contemporary rural use of Scots but with despair and contempt on the vibrant urban Scots of the poor. In the twentieth century, armed with grammars, national examinations and standardised teaching, they began a sustained assault on the remaining use of Scots, aided by growing literacy and the greater availability of newspapers, radio, gramophones, cinema and television. Growing up in Glasgow, Mrs Purvis across the road from me had a steady stream of after-school pupils each day attending her elocution lessons – having their glottal stops extracted, **oxters** turned into armpits.

Despite – or perhaps because of – this, there thrived a Scots language culture, vibrant, if **tartanry**, in the Saturday-night music-hall entertainment of ordinary working folk, with performers such as Harry Lauder able to reach out to millions not only at home but in Canada and especially Australia.

A renaissance of Scots in literature, strongly allied to a resurgence of nationalist politics and the very media that had helped standardise the language, also preserved its words, accents, stories and culture, from *Para Handy* to *Still Game*.

A key figure in the history of modern Scots is Billy Connolly. The Big Yin bestrides our recent culture like a colossus. Rooted in urban poverty, he worked in the shipyards of the Clyde, moonlighting as a folk singer and gradually telling stories in between singing traditional songs. This brought him into contact with artists, musicians and poets working within the finest traditions of Scottish culture, including the Shetland fiddler Aly Bain, the traveller singer Belle Stewart, and poet Norman MacCaig. Integrating tradition without losing touch with his roots (whatever the '**Ah kent his faither**' detractors might have said), Connolly moved from a minor club act to a comedian who was selling out theatres, first in Scotland, then in the rest of Britain and eventually across the world; records, cartoon strips, books, plays, TV and Hollywood stardom followed. His use of Scots, if perhaps toned down to be accessible to global audiences, is still at the heart of his humour and is a vital element in how he communicates and why he makes people laugh. That humour contains within itself an intrinsic Scottishness that defines us as a people. That is why, despite all the pressures down the centuries from state, church and establishment, Scots is still used and loved by **a'body**.

But from worldwide to the local, what words can really be classed as Scottish? Is the language of Burns really a universal Scots?

Consider the amazingly popular children's picture book by Julia Donaldson that has been translated by James Robertson into *The Gruffalo in Scots*. The mouse (or moose) responds to the creatures it meets with the line, 'A gruffalo! Whit dae ye no ken?' The story has also been translated into various Scots dialects and the differences show that there is no standard way of speaking or writing Scots and using Scots words:

North-East Doric: 'A gruffalo! **Foo**, dae ye nae **ken**?'
Dundonian: 'A gruffalo? Yi mean yi **dinnae ken**?'
Orcadian: 'A gruffalo! Beuy, dae ye no **ken**?'
Shetlandic: 'A gruffalo! Oh, does du no keen?'
Glaswegian: 'A gruffalo! How, dae ye no know?'

And while Scots is a national and local language it is also clannish. Each family has its Scots word or phrases, helping to maintain or establish bonds of kinship. These can be words that are passed down – my grandmother referring to a psuedo-tartan cloth as bumbee tartan; my grandfather's braces were **galluses**; my father-in-law always wears **breeks**. Shared experiences also give rise to Scots usage: **bubblyjock** entered our family vocabulary holidaying on an Arran farm; feeling listless and under the weather we are a bit **wersh**; more **carnaptious** than **crabbit**. Any language flexes and adapts, but with all this variation is Scots a language or a series of dialects?

Then there is the issue – shared in Scotland with Gaelic and around the world in all non-English languages – of whether to integrate new words and terms in their English form or to adapt them. In the internet age do you call it a 'website' or, as some in the Scots language community do, transcribe it as 'wabsite' or 'wabsteid'?

As old ways of life **dwyne** and the people who spoke their unique languages die, it is natural to suppose that standard English replaces them. Not the case according to Robert McColl Millar who has made a study of the dialects spoken in the north of Scotland and the Northern Isles. He found that Scots rather than English is replacing Gaelic and that in the growing metropolis of Inverness there is an increase in the use of Aberdeenshire Doric among the younger generations.

At the 2019 Edinburgh Festival an exhibition was held of artworks inspired by Scottish Twitter messages. They reveal a use of language that is distinctively Scottish in its construction and usage even if the individual words are not in themselves always Scottish. They form part of that subversive, streetwise tradition of Scots, a modern urban freshness and vibrancy, that ties in with a love of expressive language, which is confidently, provocatively, joyously rude:

> This is **honkin** btw
> Specky hotdog
> Colossal **roaster**
> Massive weapon
> Zip it, ya muppet
> Hurricane **Bawbag**

So, wanting to pay tribute to the persistence and strength of the Scots language, I decided to put together a collection celebrating its uniqueness. In making my selection I have tried to cover the wide range of Scots discussed above. Around the poetry of the last millennium I have woven quotes from literature and drama to give the range of Scots language and experience. I have included some **weel-kent** faces – historical figures such as Mary, Queen of Scots, but also some surprises from *Monty Python and the Holy Grail* and *Dracula*. In addition to quotes I have also given some example phrases to illustrate and illuminate word meanings.

When choosing the 1,000 words it became both pleasingly apparent how many Scots words we use and how many I would have to omit. I have attempted to give a flavour of the diversity of words from all areas of the country, and ones I could hear being said; apologies if some of your personal or family favourites are not included.

Today the Scots language is recognised as a vital element of Scotland's culture and is fostered through numerous government-funded schemes. In schools the former obligatory learning of a Burns poem for 25 January has grown into a winter term dedicated to the celebration of a wider use of Scots and is supported by a small but vital publishing industry. Last Christmas two of the top three bestselling books in Scotland were *The*

Broons and Billy Connolly – a sign that Scots is very much surviving in the twenty-first century. This modest **quair**, I hope, will help to keep a vital part of Scotland's identity alive and flourishing.

Notes on the text

I have tried not to give too many variations of spellings of the same word, especially when the pronunciation is the same, e.g. **pawky** rather than pawkie; **dinnae** not dinny, etc. Instead sometimes the quote will have a different spelling to give a hint as to variations, e.g. **bonnie-penny**, high priced, expensive: 'A **bonny penny** she'll be for books.' Nan Shepherd, *Quarry Wood*.

In a few cases I have added a guide to pronunciation, e.g. **a'body** [*aw-buddy*], **abune** [*a-bin*].

Sometimes I have left the word within a longer sentence or verse that includes other Scots words not given an individual definition in the book. I trust that when I have done so the reader will be discerning enough to understand the meaning.

If you do find yourself struggling with a word, **dinny caw canny**, speak it out loud – you might be surprised by how naturally you say it.

ailsa cock

a', aa or **aw**   all.

> *The rank is but the guinea's stamp,*
> *The Man's the gowd for **a'** that.*
> Robert Burns, 'A Man's a Man for a' That', 1795

Aald Rock, da   to Shetlanders far from 'The Old Rock', it is their island home.

Abbot of Unreason   the irreligious leader of festivities, with roots deep in the pagan past suppressed by the Protestant Reformation in 1555.

> 'Graeme had lighted upon the stuffing of the fictitious
> paunch, which the **Abbot of Unreason** wore as a part of his
> characteristic dress.'
> Sir Walter Scott, *The Abbot*, 1820

aber   prefix to place name indicating **Pictish** origin and meaning a river mouth, e.g. Aberchurder, Aberdeen, Aberfeldy. This language is known as P-Celtic. The Gaelic equivalent is *inbhir* [*inver*].

a'body [*aw-buddy*]   everybody, used particularly in Angus, the Mearns and the north-east.

> 'Oor Wullie, your Wullie, **a'body**'s Wullie.'
> *Oor Wullie Annual*, 2017

abune [*a-bin*]   above, spoken annually the whole world over when Scots are gathered and haggis are addressed each Burns night.

> ***Aboon** them a' ye tak your place . . .*
> Robert Burns, 'Address to a Haggis', 1786

ach   universally used, expressive sound at the beginning of any number of statements. Can be long or short and indicate a variety of emotions, e.g. indignation or resignation ('**Aaach**, the **Jags** were beaten 5–1 again'). See also **och**.

Advocate   legal term for a barrister, a lawyer who pleads in the High Court. The Advocate General for Scotland (the Lord Advocate from 1707 to 1998) is the state's chief prosecutor; an Advocate Depute will prosecute in a case on his or her behalf. Since 1532 **Advocates** have been represented by the Faculty of Advocates, members of which elect their head, the Dean of the Faculty of Advocates. Scotland's independent legal system is a source of many unique words and phrases still in everyday use.

aff [*aff*]   1. off, as in the apocryphal Glasgow tram conductor's interdiction 'C'moan get **aff**!' ('Please alight from this public transportation vehicle promptly'); 2. from, as in 'Cadge a fag **aff yir grannie**' ('Borrow a cigarette or cigarillo from one's grandmother'). Combined in a single sentence both meanings might be intended: 'He's **aff** his nut **aff Buckie**' ('That chap is inebriated from quaffing fortified wine made by the monks of Buckfast Abbey').

affy   awfully, very: 'Susan Boyle's **affy braw**.' Also 'awfy' [*awe-fay*].

afore   before. 'Afore ye go' is the famous advertising strapline for Bell's whisky, implying that one should stay just a wee bit longer and enjoy a companionable **dram** before leaving. See also **deoch-an-doris.**

afterheid   the green grass that sprouts in the stubble after the harist (harvest) is gathered in.

agley   askew, askance.
> *The best-laid schemes o' mice an' men*
> *Gang aft agley.*
> Robert Burns, 'To a Mouse, On Turning Her Up in Her nest With the Plough, November, 1785', 1786

Ah kent his faither   literally: 'I knew his father.' A put-down for those who are deemed to have grown too big for their boots or who look down on their roots.

ahent/ahint   behind.

> *When I cam hame wi' the* **thrang** *o' the years* **ahint** *me . . .*
> Violet Jacob, 'The Water-Hen', 1915

aiblins   perhaps, possibly. Literary, South of Scotland word, found in Ramsay, Burns, Scott and here in a John Buchan poem:

> *But hear my dream, for* **aiblins** *you*
> *May find a way to riddle't true.*
> John Buchan, 'The Fishers', 1917

Ailsa cock or **parrot**   puffin (*Fratercula arctica*). Ailsa Craig is a rock in the Firth of Clyde where the birds nest (see also **Paddy's Milestane**). On the Bass Rock on the east coast the puffin is a Tammie Norrie.

> *Tammie Norrie o' the Bass*
> *Cannae kiss a bonnie lass.*
> Traditional

Airdrie hanky   a sleeve used instead of a handkerchief. (The location varies according to one's prejudices. Apologies to Airdrieonians – it's the term my big brother uses.) See also **snochters**.

airt   place, direction or compass direction, quarter. Most commonly used in the phrase 'airt and pairt', which indicates wholehearted involvement in the directing and carrying out of an act. In a legal context it means that a person is fully involved in both the planning and execution of a crime. See also **webster**.

airt o' the clicky   the future route of an undecided traveller being determined by the direction a balanced stick falls when let go.

Alba [*al-a-pa*] (Gaelic)   Scotland (*Albanach*, 'Scot'; *ban-Albanach*, 'Scotswoman'; *Albannach*, 'Scottish'). Since 1398 the Duke of Albany has been the title conferred on the monarch's second son.

antisyzygy   term coined by C. Gregory Smith in *Scottish Literature* (1919) that describes the supposed duality in the character of the Scots, often referred to as 'Jekyll and Hyde' from Robert Louis Stevenson's novella.

antrin   odd, unusual, rare.
> 'But there was more to it than that, some never knew it, but real enough, an **antrin** magic that bound you in one with the mind, not only the body of a man, with his dreams and desires, his loves, even hates . . .'
> Lewis Grassic Gibbon, *Grey Granite*, 1934

Arbroath smokie   haddock smoked in the North Sea fishing town (although the practice originally comes from Auchmithie, a village to the north of Arbroath). In farmers' markets along the east coast, the Spink family will demonstrate the technique with pairs of haddock hung on a pole suspended over smoking applewood in an open-ended whisky barrel, a damp sack forming the lid. Utterly delicious. See also **finnan haddie**.

Argyle (alternative spelling of Argyll)   a diamond pattern used in woollens, especially pullovers and socks; popularly worn by older, monied golfers, and latterly adopted by football hooligans known as 'casuals' after the casual wear they favour.

Argyll   Earre Ghàidheal, or 'coast of the Gaels'; West Highland district of rugged mountain, loch and coastline corresponding to the ancient Irish–Norse kingdom of Dál-Riata – the power base of the Clan Campbell whose chiefs, the dukes of **Argyll**, wielded huge influence on the history of Scotland until first the court (in 1603) and then government (1707) decanted to London.

Arrochar Alps   a dramatic mountain range in the area of Loch Long, **Argyll**, very close to Glasgow; popular with hill-walkers from the city who can get there, climb the peaks and get back home in a day with only a small financial outlay.

ashet [*ash-ett*] (French, *assiette*)   big plate or serving dish.

athegither   altogether.
> 'I thocht I'd let it lie till we discharged in the port an' get rid o't
> **athegither**.'
> Bram Stoker, *Dracula*, 1897

Athens of the North   Edinburgh, so called (mainly by Edinburghers) because of its neoclassical buildings and Enlightenment philosophers.

Atholl Brose   pudding made from oatmeal, honey, whisky and water (sometimes with the addition of double cream); reputedly dating from the Earl of Atholl suppressing a rebellion in 1475 by adding whisky and honey to a well. It is served to the Seaforth Highlanders of Canada on **Ne'er Day** morning.

Atholl Highlanders   a ceremonial unit created by Queen Victoria in 1842 and based at Blair Castle, Perthshire, the seat of the Dukes of Atholl. It is the only (legal) private army in Scotland.

aucht-day   literally: 'eighth day'. Just another day in the eternal cycle of days, weeks, months, years.

Auchtermuchty [*och-terr-muck-tay*] (Gaelic, from *auchter*, 'upland'; *muchty*, 'pigs/boars')   often believed to be a mythical construct for an atypical rural Lowland Scottish town, it is in fact a real place. Culturally vibrant, once home to squeezebox legend Jimmy Shand and folk/pop twins The Proclaimers, it hosts an annual **stovies** competition.

Auld Alliance   the relationship between Scotland and France, a natural ally to balance the power of England, especially during the medieval and early modern periods. Many French words have made their way into the Scottish vocabulary.

Auld Enemy   the adjacent kingdom of England. Contemporary use is restricted mainly to a sporting context – but England is still the enemy, obviously.

Auld Lang Syne, see **syne**.

Auld Reekie, see **reek**.

Auld Yule   the old Christmas, as marked in the old Julian calendar before the amendments by the Catholic Pope Gregory XIII in 1582, and therefore celebrated a fortnight after 25 December. Strict Scottish Protestants still adhere to the pre-Gregorian calendar. See also **two New Years**.

avizandum   legal term from the Latin *avizare*, 'to consider', meaning the time taken by a court or judge to consider a case in private before deciding how to proceed.

ay   always.
   '**Ay** fuckand lyke ane furious fornicator.'
   Sir David Lyndsay, describing King James V, sixteenth century

B

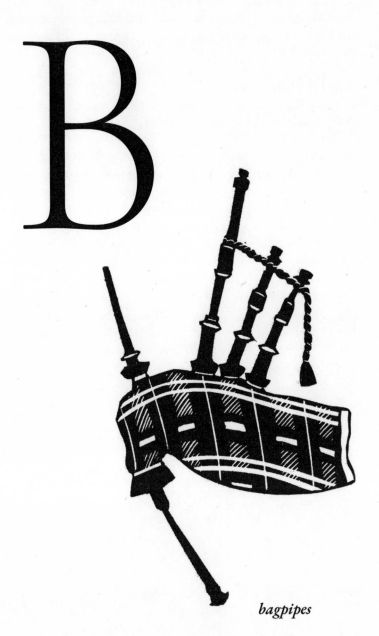

bagpipes

babbity bowster   traditionally, the last dance at a country **ceilidh** where the participants form a circle and take turns at **babbing** (bobbing) in front of their chosen partner, then kneel and exchange a kiss on a **bowster** (bolster pillow).

back green or **court**   communal area, usually grassed, at the rear of a **tenement**, used for hanging out washing and as a children's play area.

backarties   backwards, hence somersaults: 'The **bairns** in Dundee were doing **backarties** in the green when the **ingin pehs** arrived.'

bagpipes   national musical instrument of Scotland, the *Piob Mhòr*, the great Highland bagpipe, originating in the sixteenth and seventeenth centuries. In a set of Highland **bagpipes** there are five pipes: through one, air is blown from the player's mouth into a bag which is held under the **oxter**; the melody is played by the fingers on holes on the chanter (the flute-like pipe), while set notes come from the three pre-tuned drones (two tenor, one bass), which rest on the player's shoulder. The music of the pipes, often dependent on the quality of the piper, can divide opinion.

'The scheiphyrd Pan that playt to the goddis on his **bag pype**.'
The Complaynt of Scotland, 1549

'I understand the inventor of the **bagpipes** was inspired when he saw a man carrying an indignant, asthmatic pig under his arm. Unfortunately, the man-made sound never equalled the purity of the sound achieved by the pig.'
Sir Alfred Hitchcock

bahookie/behouchie   bottom, backside, bum: 'A blast o' the pipes'll get him **aff** his **bahookie**.'

baillie (Old French, *bailli*, 'bailiff')   municipal office-bearer or steward.

'Gentlemen, fill a brimmer – this is my excellent friend, **Baillie** Nicol Jarvie's health – I kend him and his father these twenty years.'
Sir Walter Scott, *Rob Roy*, 1817

bairn   literally: 'baby', but can also apply to toddler and pre-school-age children. The '**Bairn**' is the unnamed youngest child of **The Broons**. The plural **bairns** is often a universal epithet for children in general: 'We're all Jock Tamson's **bairns**.' The Bairns is the nickname of Falkirk Football Club.

balefire   1. Borders warning beacon; 2. funeral pyre. See also **Beltane**.

Balmorality   from Balmoral, the pseudo-Scottish castle holiday home of the British royal family – a show of **Scottishness** by those in positions of power, unaccompanied by any understanding of the needs or concerns of the Scottish people. See also **tartanry**.

bam/bampot   a fool or someone who behaves in a foolish manner liable to inconvenience others, such as the guy on the Glasgow–Edinburgh express who pulled the emergency brake cord when the train didn't stop at his station, forced open the doors and then wandered off down the track, bringing the whole of rush-hour commuter train travel in central Scotland to a halt.

bannock   an oatcake, traditionally baked on a **girdle**. In the east of the country a **bannock** will have a little wheat flour added to make it softer. See also **Selkirk bannock**.

Bannockburn   the battle near Stirling in 1314 between the Scots led by Robert the Bruce and the invading army of Edward I of England, resulting in the most famous victory in Scottish history and confirming Scotland as an independent nation.

barley-bree　malt liquor, whisky. See also **usquebaugh**.

The barley bree ! the barley bree !
My benison on the barley bree !
What reddens the haffets, a' brightens the ee,
Like fa' brimming bickers o' barley bree?
Song submitted to *Edinburgh Literary Journal*, signed 'W. W.', 1830

Barras, the　east end of Glasgow flea market where goods were once sold from hand barrows. While it might once have been a place to get a genuine bargain (owing to the various non-traditional supply chains of the products on offer), those days are so very long gone. 'Aye the **Barras** are better,' rang a cheery 1980s TV advert. 'Yir **maw**!' said the trading standards officers.

barrie　excellent, very good; used mainly in Edinburgh and the East of Scotland, it has its origins in the Romany tongue.

bashit　mashed, as in **bashit** neeps (turnips), served at a **Burns Supper**.

bauchle　shambling, slipshod; originally meaning a worn-down shoe, it now has various connotations of being down at heel, from an object being misshapen to a person being dishevelled.

baw/bawze　1. ball; round, as in **bawface**; 2. testicle(s).

bawbag　literally, 'scrotum', but also used to describe a low, disreputable and untrustworthy character: 'He robbed his auntie's purse when she was in the hospital, a total **bawbag**.' **Hurricane Bawbag** was a name appended to a fierce storm in December 2011 and which quickly spread, trending on social media.

bawbee　small denomination coin. Originally worth sixpence Scots (equivalent to an English halfpenny) when introduced in 1538, it was devalued by half during the reign of James VI.

bawer   beaver (*Castor fiber*).
>*Than in ane mantill and ane **bawer** hat.*
>Robert Henryson, 'Testament of Cresseid', fifteenth century

bawhair   pubic hair; commonly used as a measurement to describe a very tiny margin: 'Scotland just failed to win the World Cup by a **bawhair**.'

bawheid   a foolish person (only a **bawheid** would believe the previous quote).

beamer   a blush caused by embarrassment: 'When he asked her out, she got a total **beamer**.'

beastie   wee creature. Most famously Burns' mouse but also can refer to the frightening aspect of creeping, fast-moving or supernatural wee beasts.
>*From ghoulies and ghosties*
>*And long-leggedy **beasties***
>*And things that go bump in the night,*
>*Good Lord, deliver us!*
>Traditional prayer

beelin'   being red in the face from rage: 'When her girlfriend heard, she was pure **beelin'**.'

behouchie, see **bahookie**.

bell the cat   the nickname of Earl Archibald Douglas (father of the poet William Douglas), who, in 1482, when none of the other Scots lords would act against James III's commoner favourites, supposedly said, 'I'll **bell the cat**', and proceeded to hang his low-born rivals from a bridge.

bells, the   the stroke of midnight when bells ring to announce the New Year. See also **Ne'er Day**.

belly-huddroun   fat-bellied person.
> *My **belly huddrun**, my swete hurle bawsy* [sweet, clumsy oaf].
> William Dunbar, 'The Dance of the Sevin Deidly Synnis', *c.* 1500

belt, the, see **tawse**.

Beltane   Celtic fire festival marking the advent of spring at the beginning of May. It has recently been revived, with a torchlit procession and celebrations on Calton Hill in Edinburgh. Traditionally, it marked the moving of cattle and people to summer pastures in rural communities. They returned around **Samhain** at the end of October. See also **balefire**.

besom [*biz-zum*]   1. a broom made out of twigs bound at the end of a pole, hence also ... 2. a badly behaved female, implying witchiness, often used to describe a young woman or girl: 'Oh, she's a cheeky **besom**, that yin.'

bevvy   a beverage, alcoholic; almost always plural, and collectively can indicate a number of beverages consumed with friends over the course of an evening/day/weekend or longer period that might have begun with the intention to have only a '**wee bevvy**'.

bide   live, reside, stay.
> *For we're no awa' tae **bide** awa'*
> *we're no awa' tae leave ye,*
> *For we're no' awa' tae **bide** awa',*
> *We'll aye come back an' see ye.*
> Traditional farewell song

bidie-in   a live-in partner and/or lover.

bile   boil, as in 'Awa' an' **bile** yer **heid**!'

bing   a large mound or deposit of debris from industrial mining in the nineteenth and twentieth centuries, such as the red-shale **bings** in West Lothian. See also **blaes**.

birk   birch tree. Birches – sometimes copper but for the most part silver – thrive in the damp, boggy and mountainous conditions of Scotland, spectacularly so in locations such as the **Birks** of Aberfeldy, Perthshire.

blabs   nettle stings; also sometimes chickenpox.

black-affrontit   severely embarrassed or ashamed: 'He walked down the aisle o' the **kirk** wi' the back o' his **kilt** tucked intae the belt o' his **sporran** – the bride wis **black-affrontit**.' See also **scramble**.

black bun   extremely dense cake made with currants, raisins and nuts encased in pastry, served or gifted as a **first foot** at **the bells** and **Ne'er Day**.

Black Watch   part of the militia established from Highland clans in the early eighteenth century to guard against cattle rustling and rebellion. Some would say the soldiers' hearts were as dark as their **tartan** uniforms. As with most other Scottish regiments, a list of the **Black Watch**'s battle honours is a potted history of the rise and fall of the British Empire. It survives currently as a battalion in the Royal Regiment of Scotland.

blackhouse (Gaelic, *taigh dubh*)   traditional dwelling house of the Highlands and Islands with double dry-stone walls, reed-thatch and a beaten earth floor with a hearth at the centre. The peat smoke from the hearth could escape only through the roof, hence the name **blackhouse**. Usually housed crofting families, as well as their cattle in winter.

blaes   compressed and burned waste from collieries (see **bing**). Red-ash blaes was used as an all-weather surface for school football pitches following the Second World War. Its ability to hurt and maim children seeking youthful pleasure at play gave it a particular Scottish character, and it is surely responsible for ensuring failure at our national game for generations to come.

blast   1. violent wind; 2. blow on a trumpet; 3. vanity, blowing one's own trumpet. Notoriously, all three meanings appear in the polemic *The First Blast of the Trumpet Against the Monstrous Regiment of Women* published by John Knox in 1558. It is, however, used more tenderly by Burns.

> *Oh wert thou in the **cauld blast**,*
> *On yonder lea, on yonder lea;*
> *My **plaidie** to the angry **airt**,*
> *I'd shelter thee, I'd shelter thee.*
> Robert Burns, 'Oh wert thou in the cauld blast', *c.* 1770

blatherskate   someone who talks too much or imprudently. A 'blether' is a softer version of the same, or the gossipy chat between people: 'Ah wis jist hae'in a wee blether with Mrs McScruttock aboot the West Lothian Question.'

blaws snell   a biting, chastening wind.

bleezin'   1. bragging; 2. drunk. **Bleezin' fou** is very, very drunk.
'And ye'll specially understand that ye're no to be **bleezing** and blasting about your master's name or mine.'
Sir Walter Scott, *Rob Roy*, 1817

blithemeat   food or meal given to celebrate the birth of a child.

blooter   1. very, very drunk: 'He's totally **blootered** on Blue Label'; 2. to kick very hard: 'The **Blue Brazil** haud a chance tae win the cup but he **blootered** the ba' o'er the bar!'

bluebell (*Hyacinthoides non-scripta*)   one of Scotland's national flowers, with associations with fairies and witches in folklore. These lines appear in *The Scots Musical Museum* in 1803:

> *O where and O where does your highland laddie dwell;*
> *He dwells in merry Scotland where the **blue bells** sweetly*
> *smell . . .*

But with the Napoleonic Wars raging, they were soon adapted to:
> *Oh, where, and oh, where is my highland laddie gone,*
> *He's gone to fight the French, for King George upon the throne,*
> *And it's oh in my heart I wish him safe at home.*

Blue Brazil nickname of Cowdenbeath Football Club, whose Wikipedia entry reads, 'The club has never won any of the major honours in Scottish football.'

boak vomit (noun and verb). If someone's words or actions are appalling – or especially self-seeking – one might comment, 'Does that no gie ye the dry **boak**?'
> *May God damn an' blast an' pit a pox on pious folk.*
> *Ah loathe an' detest them they gie me the **boke**.*
> Liz Lochhead, *Tartuffe*, 2002

body o' the kirk the centre of a gathering: 'C'mon intae the **body o' the kirk**' is an invitation to join a party.

bogey the cancellation of a children's game before the scheduled end.
> 'That game was a **bogey**. Pub rules, son, if a game doesn't get
> finished all bets are cancelled.'
> James Kelman, *A Chancer*, 1987

boggin' dirty, horrible. From the Gaelic *bogach*, meaning 'bog'.

bogie 1. substance excavated from the nose: 'Eatin' yir ain **bogies** is **boggin**''; 2. a cart constructed by children out of old wood and boxes, steered using clothes rope and powered by gravity, to hurtle down hills, often resulting in injury; 3. a popular roll of tobacco, manufactured originally in Keith on the River Bogie in the nineteenth century.

***Bogey** roll, the only tobacco with a sufficient kick in it.*
Harry Lauder, 'Roamin' in the Gloamin'', 1911

bonnet laird   a small-scale farmer who owns his or her own land.
'It was better at Hermiston, where Kirstie Elliott, the sister of
a neighbouring **bonnet-laird**, and an eighteenth cousin of the
lady's, bore the charge of all, and kept a trim house and a good
country table.'
Robert Louis Stevenson, *Weir of Hermiston*, 1896

bonnie   pretty, handsome, attractive.
*I love a lassie, a **bonnie** Hielan' lassie.* [female]
Harry Lauder, 'I Love a Lassie', 1907

*My **Bonnie** lies over the ocean*
*My **Bonnie** lies over the sea*
*My **Bonnie** lies over the ocean*
*Oh, bring back my **Bonnie** to me.* [male]
Traditional (referring to **Bonnie** Prince Charlie)

'The **Bonnie** Banks o' Loch Lomond' [neuter]
Traditional

bonnie-penny   high priced, expensive.
'A **bonny penny** she'll be for books.'
Nan Shepherd, *The Quarry Wood*, 1928

bonspiel (Flemish, *bollen spel* – see the painting *The Hunters in the
Snow* (1565) by Pieter Bruegel the Elder)   a **curling** match between
numerous teams and clubs, traditionally played only when winter freezes
lochs hard enough to support the weight of so many players.

bonxie   Shetland name of Norse origin for the great skua (*Stercorarius
skua*), a large seabird, which has now entered common parlance among
naturalists as a trope.

bool   child's marble. To have '**bools** in **yir** moo' is to affect speaking with an upper-class accent.

Border, the   Scotland's only land border, that with England. The marching song of the army regiment the King's Own Scottish Borderers went:

Stand to your arms then, and march in good order;
England shall many a day
Tell of the bloody fray,
*When the Blue Bonnets came over the **Border**.*
Sir Walter Scott, 'Blue Bonnets Over the Border', *c.* 1800

bothan [*baw-can*] (Gaelic)   unlicensed – and thus illegal – drinking place, especially in the Highlands and Islands. Strict Presbyterian influence allied with the public-health concerns of members of local authority licensing boards limited the number of pubs and hotels able to offer an alcoholic drink, resulting in **bothans**, particularly in the period following the Second World War.

bothy   originally, communal accommodation for agricultural workers hired on a season-by-season basis; now, basic accommodation in remote locations for free use by outdoor walkers, hikers and cyclists.

bowffin'   unpleasant, rank: 'Yon week-old curry is pure **bowffin'**.'

brae   hill (as opposed to 'ben', meaning 'mountain'); occurs in place names such as Braemar in Aberdeenshire or Electric **Brae** in Ayrshire (where an optical illusion reverses normal perceptions so that when going downhill it appears you are travelling uphill and vice versa).

brammer   a very fine fellow: '**Wee** Bertie's a **brammer**.'

branks   a scold's bridle. In 1567 in Edinburgh, Bessie Telfer was sentenced to be '**brankit**' and chained to the **mercat cross** for slandering Baillie Thomas Hunter. She had accused him of selling her short measures.

braw   good, fine: 'It's a **braw** bricht moonlicht nicht the nicht.' In the Borders a **Braw Lad** and **Braw Lass** are elected at the Braw Lads Gathering in Galashiels each summer, an event celebrating the town's burgh charter in 1599.

breeks   trousers; **nerra breeks** are narrow trousers.

breenge   to plunge and rush, carelessly.
   time prismed to language's muckle flaws
   & need for a never-ending breenge
   Stuart A. Paterson, 'Breenge', 2016

bridie   meat pastry made in Forfar, sometimes with onion; popular in the *boulangeries* of Dundee as testified by the famous phrase, 'Twa **bridies**, ples. A plen an an' an **ingin** an an' a'.' [A pair of Forfarshire meat pastries, please. A plain one and an onion one as well.]

Brigadoon   mid-twentieth-century musical and Hollywood film, centred on a mythical Scottish village; synonymous with a false and idealised vision of Scotland's past, and **tartanry**.

broch   Iron Age defensive structure. About two thousand years old, **brochs** are built of stone, double walled and found in coastal areas, predominantly in the western and northern Highlands and Islands. They were probably occupied for only short periods of danger by the small communities that constructed them. The finest extant example is at Mousa in Shetland but most are now in a ruinous state.

Broons, The   a massively popular cartoon strip of this most quintessentially Scottish family running in the *Sunday Post* since 1936, with a compendium of stories issued in book form every two years. Maw and Paw Broon have eight children; some, like their parents, have no first names – the Twins, the **Bairn** – but no one seems to mind this and the many other idiosyncrasies of the family from Glebe Street. National treasures.

brownie   a (usually) kindly and domestic supernatural creature with a gruff Scots sense of humour.

bubblyjock   turkey. I first heard this word when holidaying on a farm in Arran that had a big old **bubblyjock** as a pet. The farmer told me they bought it for the pot but had grown so fond of it that it had survived many a Christmas.

Buckie   nickname for Buckfast, the brand name of a tonic wine, 15 per cent proof, with added caffeine; made by Benedictine monks at Buckfast Abbey, Devon, and popular with Scotland's younger and less discerning drinker. A glass a day is said to improve health.

bumfle   a wee bump or crease that needs smoothing.
> 'No, I always have a **bumfle**,' she said, reaching up her sleeve for a handkerchief.
> 'Bumfle?'
> 'It's an old word for the lump a hanky makes in your sleeve,' she said.
> Kimberley Freeman, *Evergreen Falls*, 2015

bunnet   a cap or bonnet. A blue **bunnet** was an identifier of a Lowland Scot (see **the Border**). Another **bunnet** coming over the border is celebrated in this poem marking the election of the first Labour MP.
> *The man wi' a **bunnet** t' cover his pate,*
> *Wi' a braid **Scotch** tongue and a cause to relate,*
> *He gar'd them sit up and made them tak heed*
> *For a cause that was just – some day would succeed.*
> John Reston, 'In Memory of Keir Hardie Entering the House of Commons', *c.* 1895

Burns Night   a genuinely national and international annual celebration on 25 January of the birthday of Robert Burns (1759–1796), ploughman poet, bard of Scotland. As both a poet and a collector of traditional song, he has probably been the greatest single influence on the preservation, survival and continued use of the Scots language.

'They spak their thoughts in plain braid **lallans**, like you or me.'

Robert Burns, letter to W. Simpson, 1785

Burns Supper   a dinner given to celebrate the life and works of Robert Burns on **Burns Night**. A treasure chest of the Scots language, from the food eaten – such as **haggis** and **bashit** neeps – **drams** drunk, graces spoken, poems recited and songs sung.

Fair fa' your honest, sonsie face,
Great chieftain o the puddin'-race!
Aboon them a' ye tak your place,
Painch, tripe, or thairm . . .

Robert Burns, 'Address to a Haggis', 1786

but an' ben   a twentieth-century, two-roomed dwelling, possibly once home to a **cottar**, now more likely to be a holiday home for younger generations of the **cottar**'s family, disappearing as a recognisable building type as a result of home improvements, extensions and age. The **ben** was the main living, eating and sleeping room and the **but** (abutment) an added-on kitchen or outhouse.

buttery, see **rowie**.

by the way   slightly aggressive Glaswegian addition to the end of a sentence to emphasise an assertion or statement therein. Well, that's my definition, **by the way**.

byke   1. wasp's nest or wild bee's hive; 2. nose, beak.

'He has a young Irish wife, a wasp came buzzing to her at dinner; [he] got out with hot water, a sieve and his Irish groom; and nobly, tho' with some stings, destroyed the whole **byke**.'

Thomas Carlyle, letter to Jane Welsh Carlyle, 1852

C

creel

cabbieclaw (French, *cabillaud* or Dutch, *kabeljau*)   cod in an egg and horseradish sauce.

> 'Captain Edward Topham, who visited Scotland in 1774 and wrote a vivid account of Edinburgh life, greatly enjoyed a dish called Cabbie-Claw, which he described as "cod-fish salted for a short time and not dried in the manner of common salt fish; and baked with parsley and horse radish. They eat it with egg-sauce, and it is extremely luscious and palatable".'
>
> Annette Hope, *A Caledonian Feast*, 2002

caber   tree trunk or substantial wooden pole, approximately 6 metres in length and 80 kilos in weight; used as a trial of physical strength at Highland Games, **tossing the caber**, it is propelled end over end by contestants.

caberfeidh [*kabber-fay*] (Gaelic)   the antlers of a deer; it is associated with the MacKenzies, who have it as their clan crest and shout it as their war cry or **slogan**.

cadge   borrow, scrounge. A **cadger** is someone who borrows or begs, hence also a beggar or peddlar. Cadger's news is old news (as is piper's or fiddler's news).

cailleach [*kall-ee-yock*] (Gaelic)   old woman; also associated with the ancient mother goddess. On Ben Cruachan, above Loch Awe in **Argyll**, the *Cailleach Bheur*, or Old Hag of the Ridges, is still said to control the weather on the mountain.

CalMac   Caledonian MacBrayne. Publicly owned Clyde Coast and Hebridean ferry operator with roots deep in the Highland and Island culture. With the mountain and sea loch geography of Scotland's west coast, ferry travel remains integral to transportation logistics – commercial, domestic and tourist – as referenced in this version of Psalm 24.

> *The Earth belongs unto the Lord*
> *And all that it contains*

Except the Clyde and the Western Isles
And they are all MacBrayne's.

Calcutta Cup   trophy presented to the winner of the Scotland v. England rugby match, first played in Kolkata, India, on Christmas Day 1872.

'It was Scotland's sporting shame of the 1980s, the night when rugby's John Jeffrey [Scotland] and Dean Richards [England] apparently played football with the **Calcutta Cup** on Princes Street.

'But as with many legendary tales, it turns out the facts are not quite as told.

'More than 20 years after the infamous incident, Jeffrey has finally revealed that the delicate 100-year-old cup was not kicked down Princes Street, but was dropped after being used as a makeshift rugby ball.'

The Scotsman, 28 June 2010

Caledonia   the Latin name for Scotland. The Roman historian Tacitus uses it to describe the land beyond the line of the rivers Clyde and Forth.

'The peoples inhabiting **Caledonia** embarked . . . on an unprovoked assault on a fort, and the fact that they were the challengers had caused additional dread.'

Tacitus, *Agricola*, 98 CE

caller   fresh; featured in this well-known Edinburgh fishwives' song.
*Wha'll buy my **caller** herrin*
They're bonnie fish and halesome farin,
*Wha'll buy my **caller** herrin,*
New drawn frae the Forth.

caman (Gaelic)   wooden stick with curved end for hitting the ball, used in the Highland sport of **shinty** (or 'camanachd'). **Caman** has its roots in the Gaelic word for 'curved' and can apply to a **shinty** or hurling stick or even a **golf** club.

camstairy or **camsteerie**   1. (of a person) awkward and mettle-some, ready to argue and dispute; 2. (of a place) disordered, overturned, messy.

*Yon auld **camsteerie** ghaistlie place ...*
Edwin Morgan, *The Whittrick*, 1973

Candlemas, see **quarter days**.

cannae   cannot.
*Yi **cannae** shove **yir grannie aff** a bus.*
Traditional children's song, sung to the tune of 'She'll Be Coming Round the Mountain'.

canny   shrewd, cautiously wise. To 'ca' **canny**' is to proceed warily.

cantrip   1. tricky, unnatural, supernatural; 2. a spell or magic trick.
Coffins stood round, like open presses,
That shaw'd the dead in their last dresses;
*And by some develish **cantraip** slight,*
*Each in its **cauld** hand held a light.*
Robert Burns, 'Tam o'Shanter', 1790

capercailzie   a bird of the grouse family. Found mainly in the pine forests of the Cairngorms. At the 'lek', the competitive gathering to win the most females with which to mate, the large, black, turkey-sized males hold out their wings, fan their tails and with upstretched necks make a series of distinctive clicks ending in a popping sound. In this state they are notoriously fearless of anything, including humans and, in a famous BBC film, even a Land Rover.

carnaptious   grumpy. See also **crabbit**.

cairy-oot   a selection of alcoholic beverages to be drunk away from the licensed premises in which they were purchased.

carse   low-lying, fertile land, usually between a line of hills and a river estuary, such as the **Carse** of Gowrie or Kerse Road, Stirling.

cateran (Gaelic, *ceatharn*)   cattle rustler. The **Cateran** Trail through Perthshire is a modern-day walk that follows the route taken by some of the Highland raiding parties from the fifteenth to seventeenth century.

'A party of Caterans have come down upon us last night, and have driven off all our milch cows.'
Sir Walter Scott, *Waverley*, 1814

cauld   cold. **Cauld kail** is dull food eaten by the impoverished. **Cauld kail het agin** is old news reheated. See also **blast**.

causey   causeway, road.

'But in those days, the streets were not paved at the sides, but only in the middle, or, as it was called, the crown of the **causey**; which was raised and backed upward, to let the rain-water run off into the gutters.'
John Galt, *The Provost*, 1822

ceilidh (Gaelic)   originally, an informal domestic meeting, gathering or visit where gossip, news, stories, poems and songs could be exchanged, perhaps with some dancing; now a more formalised activity with Scottish country dancing, often as part of a wedding celebration or at **Hogmanay**.

ceòl beag [*kye-oll bay-ig*] (Gaelic)   literally, 'little music' for **bagpipes**, for **strathspeys**, marches and reels. Other genres include ceòl meadhonach [*kye-oll mee-on-ach*], 'middle music' – slow marches, folk songs, lullabies (yes, lullabies, on the pipes) – and ceòl mór [*kye-oll more*], 'big music', for commemorations, laments, salutes.

ceud-mille-failte [*ki-ool-a-meel-a-fell-cha*] (Gaelic)   a greeting, literally, 'a hundred thousand welcomes'.

chanty   chamber pot. A **chunty heid** is a fool. See also **gardyloo**.

chap   to knock: 'Chap the door'.

chaser   a beer drunk after drinking a **dram**. See also **hauf an' a hauf**.

chaud melle (French, *chaud mêlée*)   literally, 'hot affray'. A former defence in Scots law for a crime committed in the passion of the moment rather than with premeditation.

chauve   work away mundanely, as in the mainstay **Doric** greeting and response: 'Foo's yer doos?' 'Jist **chauvin**' awva', **chauvin**' awva'.'

chib   heavy (non-military) weapon used to bash or club an opponent; can also be used as a verb: 'I'm goannae **chib** youse.'

chief   the head of a **clan** under the old system.
>   *Nor slept thy hand by thy side, **chief** of the isle of mist! many*
>   *were the deaths of thine arm, Cuthullin, thou son of Semo!*
>   James Macpherson, *The Poems of Ossian*, 1765

chieftan   1. head of a branch of a Highland **clan**; 2. head of a **Highland Games**, honorary post. Formerly the **chieftan** would select his soldiers from the best performers; nowadays they are expected to hand out prizes and smile beneficently throughout the (long) day of sport, dancing and local gossip. See also **haggis**: 'Great **chieftan** o' the pudding race!'

chitter   shiver with cold or fear so that one's teeth chatter. **Chitterin'** bite is food eaten immediately after swimming in the sea or wild swimming.

clabber (Gaelic, *clavar*)   filth, dirt, mud; especially in the south-west.

Clackmannanshire   a fascinating combination of languages makes up the name of Scotland's 'wee county': *clach*, Gaelic for 'stone'; *Mannan* from the Brythonic/Pictish tribe the Manaw; and 'shire' from English.

claim call-out for a fight: 'You're **claimed**, pal!'

clan family. The ancient tribal form of governance was based on family. It was suited to the geography of the Scottish Highlands, hence the preponderance of names beginning with **'mac'** (son of) or 'nic' (daughter of). It came to an end with the suppression of the **Jacobite** rising of 1745.

clanjamfrie a to-do.
> [stage direction]: *Something of a pause.*
>> 'It's not you.
>> 'You're fine.
>> 'It's the whole . . .
>> *He makes a gesture with his hands suggesting the world is jumbled up.*
>> **'Clanjamfrie.'**
> David Greig, *Pyrenees*, 2005

clap pat. To 'gie a **cuddy** a **clap**' is to pat a horse.

clapshot a heady mix of **bashit** neeps and **tatties**.

clart dirt, mud: 'I fell in the bog cutting peats, I'm totally **clartit**.'

clavie remnant of an ancient fire ritual to welcome the New Year on the Moray coast. On **Hogmanay** a burning torch was carried around boats for good luck, purification or **saining**. In the town of Burghead it is a flaming barrel carried on a pole that still welcomes in **Ne'er Day**.

claymore Highland long sword (literally, 'big sword'). In an example of how languages and cultures interact and borrow from each other, *Claymore* is also a series of Japanese manga and anime featuring silvereyed witch warriors armed with **claymores**.

Clearances the 'clearing' of people from their traditional communities, farms and lands, often to be replaced by sheep as part of the drive for agricultural 'improvement' in the late eighteenth and nineteenth centuries in both the Highlands and Lowlands, resulting in mass emigration to the industrial cities, the New World and Australasia.

cleg   horse fly, a biting insect second only to the **midge** in terms of annoyance.

> 'I've been bit. I've been bit. I'm being bit everywhere.'
> I ran towards her and was immediately stung on the side of the neck.
> '**Clegs**,' I yelled.'
> Agnes Owens, *Like Birds in the Wilderness*, 1987

clipe/clype   tell-tale, especially in school:

> 'Ye maunna **clype** on us, Mary, fin ye gang hame.'
> *The Scottish Education Journal*, Vol. 27, 1944

clishmaclaver   the passing on of idle gossip, sometimes in a book.

clockwork orange, the   affectionate nickname for Glasgow's diminutive underground rail system.

> 'We like our Underground. From down below it tells you a lot about what is happening up above.'
> Douglas Corrance and Ian Archer, *Glasgow from the Eye in the Sky*, 1988

clootie dumpling   suet and dried-fruit pudding wrapped tightly in a cloth, or **cloot**, and cooked by being boiled in a pot.

cludgie   toilet, lavatory.

> 'This, the **cludgie**, was usually out on the landing.'
> Glenn Chandler, *Taggart's Glasgow*, 1989

collieshangie   a row or fight with two people barking at each other.

collops   thin sliced or minced meat.

'Minced **collops** may be baked in the oven, or first stewed then baked. They will keep for some time, if packed in a jar and covered like potted meats. Hare, venison and veal **collops** are prepared as above with the seasonings appropriate to each.'
F. Marian McNeill, *The Scots Kitchen*, 1929

common riding, see **marches**.

cooncil an adjective used to denote basic services: **cooncil juice** is water; **cooncil TV** is free-to-air services – the implication is of poverty preventing a person paying for more (though not necessarily better quality) channels.

coorie warm, cosy way of living with feel-good factor. Scottish equivalent of the Danish *hygge*, though its use seems to have the opposite effect on some Scots language 'purists'.

Corbett, see **Munro**.

corbie crow, raven or carrion crow (*Corvus*).
As I was walkin' a' alane
*I saw twa **corbies** makin' a mane,*
Yin untae the ither did say:
'Whaur shall we gang an' dine the day?'
Traditional, 'The Twa Corbies', possibly sixteenth century

cornkister a comic song. See **nicky-tams** for an example.

coronach (Gaelic) lament.
'The [woman singing the coronach] followed the body, every now and then striking the coffin with her hands like a drum and making all the din possible, and keeping time with the movements of the men (i.e. the bearers). All the virtues of the dead, and a few more, were mentioned and extolled, and the genealogy for many generations praised and lauded.'
Alexander Carmichael, *Carmina Gadelica*, 1900

corp criadh [*cor cree-ah*] (Gaelic; literally, 'clay body')   pagan doll effigy into which pins were stuck or from which limbs were broken to cause ill to an enemy.

corrieneuchin'   a *tête-à-tête*; close, private conversation.
> *He gave me the meaning of words*
> *like pantile, like **corrieneuchin'**. He wooed them*
> *from their lair in the dictionary.*
> Norman MacCaig, 'Two Thoughts of MacDiarmid in a Quiet Place', 1980

cottar   small independent farmer. Robert Burns' idea of a rural family gathered round while the father reads the Bible is perfectly captured in Sir David Wilkie's painting *The Cotter's Saturday Night* (1837).

coup   originally, a cart for carrying manure; now, 1. (verb) to tip up or over; 2. (noun) a dump or municipal recycling centre.

coupon   face.
> 'Big Durkin fae the Toonheid gave me this twelve-stitcher but you should've seen his **coupon** – butcher's windae stuff . . .'
> Jeff Torrington, *Swing Hammer Swing!*, 1992

Covenanter   A person who signed the National League and Covenant in the seventeenth century offering obedience to God over the king in religious affairs. The resultant schism in the Protestant Church has meant that the Church of Scotland, unlike the Church of England, is not the established church.

covin tree   a meeting place under a tree where welcomes would be made, farewells taken and agreements struck.

crabbit   grumpy; the Scots word most likely to be encountered on a mug, tea towel or apron in a bargain tourist outlet. See also **carnaptious**.
> *Thare saw I crabbit Saturn ald and haire.*
> William Dunbar, 'The Golden Targe', *c.* 1510

crack   talk, conversation; perhaps taking place in a bar, possibly with an **export** or over a **dram** or **hauf an' hauf**.

craig   rock. Ailsa **Craig** is an island in the Firth of Clyde where **curling** stones are quarried; Abbey **Craig** near Stirling is the rocky promontory on which the Wallace Monument stands.

cranachan   a delicious pudding made from layers of toasted oats, raspberries and cream with a measure of whisky added.

crannog   defensive Iron Age wooden dwelling, thatched with heather and built on log piles in the foreshore of many of Scotland's lochs. A reconstructed **crannog** can be visited near Kenmore on Loch Tay. Many of the small tree-covered islands on Scotland's lochs are actually the remnants of these **crannogs**.

crappit heids   dish of fish heads stuffed with lobster. Another example of Scottish Jekyll-and-Hyde duality.

craw-step gable   a Scottish architectural style in which blocks of squared stone are placed one on top of another, like steps, at the top of the gable ends of buildings, showing influence of the Low Countries and the Baltic states.

craw's croose   self-congratulatory boasting.

creel   a woven basket for carrying, for example, peat or fish, or used by inshore fishers for catching shellfish. The image of a multitasking woman knitting while carrying a **creel** piled high with cut peat is a quintessential image of Victorian Scotland. See also **Grannie Scotland**.

creeling   a traditional Lowland and **Borders** pre-nuptial celebration for bride or groom involving dressing up, similar to a hen or stag night. Anyone encountering the bride-to-be would, in return for a wedding gift deposited in her **creel**, receive a kiss.

croft   traditional self-sufficient farmstead, primarily in the Highlands and Islands, with secured tenure and rights for crofters.

cuddy   horse. A **Scotch cuddy** is a donkey.

cundy   drain, conduit; especially in Dundee: 'Crivens. Hen Broon's slipped doon the **cundy!**'

curling   winter game played by sliding heavy stones across ice, traditionally a frozen loch, towards a target. See also **bonspiel**, **kiggle-kagle**, **roaring game** and **soop**.

curse of Scotland   the nine of diamonds in a pack of playing cards. Various historical explanations have been offered, but the most common is that the design resembles the coat of arms of the Dalrymple family, which was associated with the Massacre of Glencoe, the Union of the Parliaments and anti-Jacobitism.

cushie-doo   turtle dove, love pigeon: 'Check the pair o' them, **cushie-doos** an' no' a day under sixty.'

cutty   white, porcelain white. A **cutty sark** is a pale white vest made famous in Burns' poem 'Tam o'Shanter'. Later, the name of a fast tea-clipper now moored in London, and a famous brand of blended whisky.
> Her **cutty sark**, o' Paisley harn,
> That while a **lassie** she had worn,
> In longitude tho' sorely scanty,
> It was her best, and she was **vauntie**.
> Robert Burns, 'Tam o'Shanter', 1790

cutty stool, see **stool of repentance**.

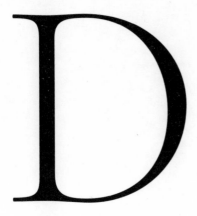

dirk

daft days   youthful, carefree days, especially around Christmas and **Hogmanay**.

'The **daft days** (as we call New Year time) passed – the days of careless merriment.'

Neil Munro, *The Daft Days*, 1907

Dashing White Sergeant   a progressive Scottish country dance or **reel** popular at **ceilidhs**, for groups of six people.

daud/dod   a piece, bit or slice; a universally adaptable word to describe a small amount of any material: 'An' while yir **daunerin'**, get us a wee **daud** o' wood.'

dauner   casual walk or glance, dander: 'Take a **dauner** doon there . . .'

deasil   clockwise, considered lucky. See also **widdershins**.

'At marriages and baptisms they make a procession round the church, **Deasoil**, i.e. sunways.'

Thomas Pennant, *A Tour in Scotland*, 1769

deek   to look at: 'Take a **dauner** doon there and ha'e a wee **deek** at whit they're up tae wi' that **daud** o' wood.'

deid   dead.

'Be happy while yir livin', for yir a lang time **deid**.'

Old Scots proverb

deif   deaf. As my grandfather's hearing deteriorated with age he would fiddle with his hearing aid, which often emitted a piercing whine, prompting my father to shout, 'Faither, yir makin' us all **deif**!'

deil   devil.

Softly he said 'I have been swindled once,
*And if I'm swindled twice, **De'il** tak us baith.*

Robert Henryson (*c.* 1460–1500), 'Moral Fables'

deil's darning needle   dragonfly (*Anisoptera*).

den   a wooded gorge or ravine with a burn or river flowing through it.
*As she went down yon **dowy den**,*
Sorrow went before her, O;
She saw her true-love lying slain
Upon the Braes o' Yarrow.
Traditional Border ballad, 'The Dowie Dens o' Yarrow'

deoch-an-doris [*doch-an-doris*] (Gaelic)   the drink(s) taken at the door on parting. Like the two-headed god of the doorway, Janus, who looks in both directions, there may be a 'double' taken, as one might suspect from the chorus of Sir Harry Lauder's dated song.
*Just a wee **deoch an doris**, just a wee drop, that's all.*
*Just a wee **deoch an doris** afore ye gang awa.*
*There's a wee wifie waitin' in a wee **but an ben**.*
*If you can say, 'It's a **braw** bricht moonlicht nicht',*
Then yer a'richt, ye ken.
Harry Lauder, 'Wee Deoch an Doris', 1911

dicht   wash, clean. Usually a child's face is given **a guid dicht wi a cloot** but Henryson's poem indicates that a knight's body is put in good order, dealt with respectfully, possibly washed in preparation for burial (and assumption into heaven).
The Lady murnyt and maid grit mane,
With all her mekill mycht –
'I luvit nevir lufe bot ane,
*That dulfully now is **dicht**;*
God sen my lyfe were fra me tane
Or I had seen yone sicht,
Or ellis in begging evir to gane
Furth with yone curtass knycht.'
Robert Henryson, 'The Bludy Serk', c. 1500

dinna/dinnae/disnae   do not/does not. A **clartit** child forcibly given a **dicht** by a parent might, during the course of the cleansing, continually shout, '**Dinnae!**' A more heinous crime is used to scare in this **bairns'** rhyme about the infamous murderers Burke and Hare, who sold the bodies of their victims to Dr Knox for medical research.

> *Burke and Hare*
> *They were a pair*
> *Killed a wife*
> *An'* **dinna'** *care.*
> *Then they pit her*
> *In a box*
> *Sent her* **aff**
> *Tae Dr Knox.*

dirdum   1. heavy blow; 2. punishment, scolding; 3. uproar. 'Dree the **dirdum**' means 'suffer the punishment'.

dirdy-lochrag (Gaelic, *dearc-luachrach*)   common lizard (*Zootoca vivipara*).

dirk   Highland long knife or dagger on which oaths would be sworn (see also **sgian dhu**). Dr Johnson in his 1755 *Dictionary* says it is 'an Erse word' but it is not Gaelic; the more likely source is the German *Dolch*, meaning 'dagger'.

dirl   resonate and vibrate, tingle.

> 'The fiercest joy of his life was the **dirl** that went up his arm.'
> George Douglas Brown, *The House with the Green Shutters*, 1901

dish of spurs   a **Border reiver**'s wife would serve his spurs on an empty plate when the cupboard was bare.

disjaskit   weary, run down, dilapidated.

Disruption   the schism in the Church of Scotland in 1843 resulting in the formation of the Free Church of Scotland, whose congregations practise a more austere, Calvinist form of Presbyterianism, particularly in the Highlands and Islands.

Dod/Doddie   diminutive or **tee-name** of someone called George; for example, rugby-player Doddie Weir.

dog   play truant.
> 'I don't like you **dogging** school,' Iris said and Pamela ignored her . . . Pamela no longer pretended to go to school, wearing her uniform to leave the house and changing at a friend's house.'
> Alison Irvine, *This Road is Red*, 2011

dominie (Latin, *dominus*, 'lord')   teacher.
> 'The **dominie** was not much troubled by the school inspector.'
> J. M. Barrie, *Auld Licht Idylls*, 1888

Donald, see **Munro**.

doo   dove, pigeon (*Columbidae*); doocot, dovecot. See also **cushie-doo**.
> 'It's jist like sma' sheepbells – fairy-sheep, I reckon, Maggy, my **doo**.'
> George MacDonald, *David Elginbrod*, 1863

dook/douk   plunge into water. **Dookin'** for apples is played at Hallowe'en. Contestants have to grab with their teeth one of the apples floating in a basin of water. Sometimes the water is swirled to make it more difficult and a contestant's head can be pushed underwater as they attempt to secure an apple. **Loony dookers** are those unhinged enough to swim in the sea, loch or river on **Ne'er Day** morning. **Dookit folk** are Baptists.

doon the watter   a trip or holiday taken – usually by boat – from Glasgow down the river to the **Firth** of Clyde. See also **Fair**.

Doric   the language and dialect of the north-east of Scotland. Its honest native purity gave rise to its comparison to the Dorians of early Ancient Greece. See also **chauve**.

> 'It is as if the **Doric** had been invented by a cabal of
> scandal-mongering beldams, aided by a council of observant
> gamekeepers.'
> George Malcolm Thomson, *The Rediscovery of Scotland*, 1928

douce (French, *douce*, 'sweet')   neat, tidy.

dough school   a college of domestic science: 'Ma **grannie** learned to cook singit [singed] **sheep's-heid** and **haggis** at the dough school.'

doup/dowp   backside, bottom: 'She fell right oan her **dowp**.'

dour   miserable and sullen, unimaginatively grim; a defining Scottish characteristic.

dovekie   black guillemot.

dowie   sorrowfully, melancholy. See also **den**.

dowt   cigarette end: 'Nae fags, I'm scoorin' the ashtrays fur **dowts**.'

dram   a measure of whisky. Ostensibly an eighth of a fluid ounce, but to measure precisely would be to offend. See also **usquebaugh**.

drappie   a wee drop of something alcoholic. A **wee drappie** could be a **dram**.

> *Job in his lamentation said man was made tae mourn,*
> *That there's nae such thing as pleasure frae the cradle to the urn;*
> *But in his meditation Job surely had forgot,*
> *The pleasure man derives owre a wee **drappie** o't.*
> Traditional song

draunting   dull whining speech; speaking with a sectarian tone.
> *He that speaks wi' a **drawnt** and sells with a cant,*
> *Is right like a snake in the skin of a saunt.*
> Allan Ramsay, *A Collection of Scots Proverbs*, 1736

dree one's weird   endure whatever fate has predestined for you.
> *But wha shall speak tae these fair maids,*
> *Aneath the waning moon;*
> *They maun **dree** a waesome **weird**,*
> *That never will be doone.*
> James Hogg, *Collected Novels*, c. 1830

dreep   drip. 'To **dreep**' is to slide or slither down a wall.

dreich   grey, miserable, tedious; usually applied to weather but indicative of the Scots temperament, hence it being voted Scotland's favourite word in a recent poll (or perhaps indicative of the temperaments of Scots who feel the need to participate in online polls): 'It's gey **dreich** the day.'

drone, see **bagpipes**.

drookit   soaking wet.
> 'Ye wud be fair **drookit** . . .'
> J. J. Bell, *The Wee Macgreegor*, 1903

drooth/drouth   a thirst brought on by not enough or too much alcohol; **drouthy**, thirsty.
> *And drouthy neebors, neebors meet.*
> Robert Burns, 'Tam o'Shanter', 1790

drover   a cattle driver. The **droving** tradition saw Highland cattle being walked to Lowland markets in Crieff and Falkirk over great distances. See also **hieland coo**.

drow   drizzly rain or squall.

dun (Gaelic)   fort, usually from the Iron Age (1000 BCE–500 CE). Found in many Scottish place names, for example: Dundee, Dunshalt, Moredun. See also **broch.**

dunce   bottom of the class, stupid; derived from the enemies of philosopher John Duns Scotus (*c.* 1266–*c.*1308), especially later Protestants who disliked his assertion of papal authority.

dunt   a shove, bump or hit.

dunted   a wee bit drunk.

dux (Latin, 'leader')   honorary title, given to the top academic pupil at a school.

dwam   daydream: 'Huh, yon'll never be **dux**, he's always away in a **dwam**.'

dwyne/dwynin'   dwindle/dwindling.

dyke   wall of a field. A dry-stane **dyke** is a rural wall built without mortar or cement but with great skill. To **loup** the **dyke** means to change sides, whereas a **loup** the **dyke** is a runaway.

E

elder

easter   a more easterly place, especially in reference to farms and areas of land; for example: Easter Ross, Easterhouse.

easy-oasy   in a relaxed, lazy or carefree manner; or a relaxed, lazy or carefree person.

Edinburgh rock   hard, sugary, pastel-coloured candy. Unlike conventional rock, the rod is diced into smaller cylindrical pieces and often merchandised in a box decorated with **tartan** and an image of Edinburgh castle.

ee/een   1. eye/eyes: 'Yir **ee**'s bigger nor yir wame'; 2. **ee o' the day**, midday.
>*Ye'll sit on his white hause-bane* [neck bone],
>*And I'll pike out his bonny blue **een**;*
>*Wi ae lock o his gowden hair*
>*We'll, theek* [thatch] *our nest when it grows bare.*
>Traditional, 'The Twa Corbies', possibly sixteenth century

eedle-doddle   scatterbrain, a person without initiative.

eejit   idiot, fool: 'The **eejit**'s broke his tooth – thought the castle was built on **Edinburgh rock**!'

eeksie-peeksie   well-matched or balanced, even stevens, six and two threes.

eel-drooner   someone with a special skill, though not always a useful one: '**Eeksie-peeksie**? He's an **easy-oasy eedle-doddle** o' an **eel-drooner**!'

eese   use (north-east): 'Fit **eese** is at?' ('What use is that?')

eident/eydent   watchful, trusty, diligent.
>'On my arrival (May 10th) I found Sir Walter to have rallied . . .
>One note had a postscript a parody on a sweet lyric of Burns's –

> *Dour, dour and **eident** was he,*
> *Dour and **eident but-an-ben** –*
> *Dour against their barley-water,*
> *And **eident** on the Bramah pen.'*
>
> John Gibson Lockhart, *Memoirs of the Life of Sir Walter Scott*, vol. 4,
> 1837

> 'Them that's slack in gude are **eydent** in evil.'
> Old Scots saying

eightsome reel   a Scottish country dance performed by groups of four couples, perhaps at a **ceilidh**.

elder   one of the ordained officers in a **kirk** who carry out pastoral and administrative duties and can represent the parish at higher church meetings. Cormorants, with their austere black feathers, are sometimes called **elders**.

elfhame   fairyland, sometimes hell.
> 'The Queen of **Elfhame** first appeared to her as she lay ill with child in bed. The queen asked her for a drink, and Bessie gave her it. To thank her the queen predicted Bessie's future.'
> Dane Love, *Legendary Ayrshire: Custom, Folklore, Tradition*, 2009

emmerteen   ant (*Formicidae*).

enoo   now, at this time.

Episcopal Church   Protestant Scottish Church that is governed by bishops (Greek, *epískopos*) and is part of the Anglican Communion. Members kneel to pray, hence the rhyme, 'Pisky, pisky-palians down on your knees and up again.'

ettle   plan, objective, goal.

> 'My father had a kind of **ettle** that I should marry into
> England.'
> Naomi Mitchison, *Bull Calves*, 1947

export   medium-strong Scottish beer brewed for the export market. With its red can and laughing cavalier logo, McEwan's **Export** has been a favourite for decades, its 1970s advertising jingle repetitive but still effective: 'McEwan's is the best buy, the best buy, the best buy; McEwan's is the best buy, the best buy in beer.' See also **heavy**.

F

fankle

fa' 1. fall; 2. fate.
'Kind Patie, now fair **fa'** your honest heart.'
Allan Ramsay, *Gentle Shepherd*, 1725

Faculty of Advocates, see **advocate**.

faff dither, waste time doing something pointless: 'Haw, Hamlet!
Didnae **faff** aboot, eh?'

fag-ma-fuff old woman gossip.

Fair, the agreed summer-holiday period taken by workers in a town
or municipality. See also **doon the watter**, **terr** and **trades**.

faniver (north-east) whenever. 'Fariver' is 'wherever'.

fank sheepfold; more common than houses in Lowland and Highland
glens. See **Clearances**.

fankle 1. tangle: 'Ma knitting's all in a **fankle**'; 2. flustered.: 'I'm all in
a **fankle** over ma knitting.'

fanny 1. slang, sexist, impersonal word for women used by males only
wanting women for sex; 2. someone behaving foolishly and/or annoy-
ingly. See also **fud**.
'The **gowf** is jist aboot the only thing that stoaps me fae
obsessin aboot the **fanny**' *and* 'Yir jist a big, useless **fanny**.'
Irvine Welsh, *A Decent Ride*, 2015

fantoosh (French, *fantoche*, 'puppet') flamboyantly or exuberantly
attired, pretentious; many examples to be found in Edinburgh during the
Festival. Fanny Toosh is a satirical name for a woman who is considered
above herself.

farl (Old English, *fardel*, 'a fourth part')   a quarter slice of a circular **oatcake** or **scone**.

fash   bother: '**Dinnae fash** yirsel'.'

fauld   small field enclosure that is manured by grazing cattle on it; in placenames such as Fauldhouse, Lochfaulds.

feart   afraid: 'Ah'm nae **feart** of yon **tattie bogle**.' 'Aye ye are, ya **feartie**!'

fecht   literally, 'fight', but implies a struggle, travail. 'Sair fecht' is literally a 'sore fight'; a hard task. 'Life – it's a sair **fecht**.'

fee'd   hired out. On the **quarter days** agricultural workers would **fee** themselves to a farm. The tune of 'Auld Lang Syne' is based on that of an old Lowlands melody 'I **fee'd** a lad at Michaelmas'.

feery-farry   a commotion: 'Man, he gets himsel' intae a **feery-farry faniver** an' fariver.'

feints   alcohol of a poorer quality created during whisky production that is added back into the still for redistillation.

ferlie (Old Norse, *ferligr*)   1. strange, monstrous; 2. fairy.
'Hob lived in the Border country, where they call a fairy a "ferlie", and he was herd-boy to Big Archie, a man who did a dangerous thing: he stole cattle from a ferlie.'
Mollie Hunter, *The Ferlie*, 1968

ferntickle   freckle. See also **ginger**.

ferry-louper   an incomer to the islands of Orkney; literally, 'jumped from the ferry'.

feu   a piece of land for the use of which a tenant pays an annual fee to the landowner. The **feuar** is the tenant; **feu duty** the fixed annual fee paid.

'At the head of Loch Ridden is Ormidale, where the late
Colonel Campbell built a pier and a commodious hotel, for
the convenience of **feuars** and visitors, many of the latter being
attracted by the fishing streams in the neighbourhood.'
Benjamin Disraeli, *Henrietta Temple: A Love Story*, 1837

fey   a person's heightened unnatural or otherworldly state; believed sometimes to presage death.

'The main character [in Muriel Spark's *The Ballad of Peckham
Rye*], Scots Dougal Douglas, is conveyed through the pervasive
ambivalence upon which his "**fey**" Scottishness and sexuality
appear to be construed.'
Monica Germanà, *Scottish Women's Gothic and Fantastic Writing*,
2010

ficherie   fiddly, fussy, finicky. Also 'footerie', possibly from the French *foutre*, meaning sexual intercourse.

fiddler's biddin'   a last-minute guest. A piper's bidding is a last-minute invite.

fiere   friend, equal, companion. The Scots **Makar** Jackie Kay's poem 'Fiere' was inspired by the novelist Ali Smith singing 'Auld Lang Syne' down the phone to her one **Hogmanay**.

And there's a hand my trusty fiere
And gie's a hand o' thine . . .
Robert Burns, 'Auld Lang Syne', 1788

fiery cross (Gaelic, *crann tara*)   summons from a Highland **clan chief** for warriors to assemble. A relay of runners would pass the message speedily over large distances of mountainous territory.

'On sudden Alarms, or when any Chieftain is in Distress, they
give Notice to their Clans or those in Alliance with them, by

> sending a Man with what they call the **Fiery Cross**, which is
> a Stick in the form of a Cross, burnt at the End, who send it
> forward to the next Tribe or Clan. They carry with it a written
> Paper directing them where to Assemble.'
> General Wade, *Jacobite Papers*, 1724

figmagairies   whims, idiosyncrasies.

filibeg/philibeg (Gaelic)   small or short **kilt**. *Filleag* means 'blanket' in the Beurla Reagaird, the language of the Scottish Traveller community.

> 'Others, again, still wore the Highland **philibeg**.'
> Robert Louis Stevenson, *Kidnapped*, 1886

filimore/philamore (Gaelic, *Feileadh Mòr*)   the big **kilt**, a single long length of tartan cloth used as both **kilt** and cloak. See also **plaid**.

finnan haddie   a smoked haddock. See also **Arbroath smokie**.

first foot   1. (noun) the first visitor over the threshold after **the bells** at **Hogmanay**; traditionally a tall, dark male bearing a gift, sometimes of coal or **black bun**; 2. (verb) the act of visiting on **Ne'er Day**.

firth (Norse, *fjord*)   river estuary or wide sea inlet, e.g. Firth of Forth, Firth of Lorne.

fit like?   north-east and Aberdonian greeting. See also **chauve**.

fitba   football, soccer.
> *Brissit brawnis and brokin banis,*
> *Stride, discord and waistie wanis;*
> *Crukit in eild, syne halt withal –*
> *Thir are the bewties of the **fute-ball**.*

[Torn muscles and broken bones,
Strife, discord and impoverishment;
Stooped in old age then lame as well,
Those are the beauties of football.]
Anon., sixteenth century

'What is hurting so many now is the realisation that something
they believed to be a metaphor for their pride has all along been
a metaphor for their desperation.'
Hugh McIlvanney, *McIlvanney on Football*, 1994

flair   floor: 'Dancers! Take the **flair** fur the **Dashing White Sergeant!**'

Flanders frost   cold south-easterly wind.

flapdawdron   'a tall ill-clad person' (*Dictionary of the Scottish Language*).

fleein'   1. flying; 2. drunk.
'Dean Ramsay, an eighteenth-century clergyman, tells the
story of an old lady who, lying on her deathbed, heard a
thunderstorm outside and declared, "What a nicht for me to be
fleein' through the air!"'
A. K. H. Boyd, *The Recreations of a Country Parson*, 1859

fleg   fright: 'Whit a **fleg**, I thocht it wis Nessie.'

flit   1. (verb) to move house; 2. (noun) a house move, a **flitting**.
'But having contracted debts he was unable to discharge, our
adventurer, with his wife, took what is called in Scotland a
moonlight **flitting**; and, on the night, between the 7th and 8th
of April, 1760, they set out.'
William Cobbett, *The Life of Thomas Paine*, 1797

flype   turn inside out, be two-faced.
> 'Sum flyrand, thair phisnomeis thai **flyp**' [some mocking, their physiognomies two-faced]
> Alexander Montgomerie, 'The Flyting betwixt Montgomerie and Polwart', *c.* 1585

flyte   a vicious but good-natured argument, traditionally between poets. 'The **Flyting** between Montgomerie and Polwart' was a verse duel between the two court poets Alexander Montgomerie and Patrick Hume of Polwart to win favour with King James VI. See also **flype**.

footerie/footery, see **ficherie**.

foosty   old, stale, mildewed: 'The **bannocks**'ve gone all **foosty**.'

forby(e) (German, *vorbei*)   1. by which; 2. also, plus.
> 'Except honor and keep a God; **forby** no other work can one find or lose God except by faith or unbelief.'
> Martin Luther (1483–1546), *Writings*

> 'Ay, an' **forby**, it was rale threadbare aneath the table.'
> J. M. Barrie, *A Window in Thrums*, 1889

forefochen   exhausted, knackered.
> 'The best champion amang us haes been sairly **forefochen**; not by spritely raisons, but by blauds.'
> William Craig Brownlee, *A Careful and Free Inquiry Into the True Nature and Tendency of the Society of Friends*, 1824

fou/fu   drunk (full of drink).
> *And at his elbow, Souter Johnny,*
> *His ancient, trusty, drouthy crony;*
> *Tam lo'ed him like a vera brither,*
> *They had been **fou** for weeks thegither.*
> Robert Burns, 'Tam o'Shanter', 1790

fud   vagina; but almost always used to describe someone behaving fool-ishly: 'Haw, Elmer. Dinnae be a **fud**.' See also **fanny**.

fykie   fidget, agitate, fuss.
As bees bizz out wi' angry fyke,
When plundering herds assail their byke.
Robert Burns, 'Tam o'Shanter', 1790

fyre-flaught   a flash of lightning. A **flaught** is a glimpse or sight.
'September 9th . . . being Saturday, ther was alfo mutch
thunder hard in the afternone, at which time ther was a great
raine, with **fyre-flaught** or lightning, which did fett on fyre a
ftouke of corne in the field.'
Mr John Lamont's diary, 1654

Gretna Green

gaberlunzie a tramp. It is said that King James V (1512–1542) roamed his kingdom in the guise of a beggarman and wrote a version of this song:

O, a beggar man cam' ower yon lea,
An' mony a fine tale he told me,
Seekin' oot for charity,
Will ye lodge a beggar man?

Traditional, 'The Gaberlunzie Man'

gadgie (Romany) a male; man, youth or boy.

'Travellers began coming in from all over the east Highlands to meet him – asking "Where is the Beinn Coul (the great gentleman) – the **gadgie** with the speaking machine? Shamus Mor?"'

The great folk tale and folksong collector and recorder described in Tim Neat, *Hamish Henderson: The Making of the Poet*, 2012

Gaedhealtacht [*gale-tacht*] the **Gaelic** areas or communities of Scotland.

Gael [*gail*] a person of Celtic heritage where **Gaelic** is spoken; now predominantly in the Highlands and Western Isles but previously widespread, as testified by the profusion of Gaelic placenames throughout Scotland.

Gaelic [*gal-ick*] language of the **Gaels**; one of the Celtic languages that is now spoken by only 1 per cent of the population, though – encouragingly – the decline in the youngest age group seems to be stabilising. An enclave of 4,000 Gaelic speakers exists in Canada and a smattering elsewhere in the Scottish worldwide diaspora. For the language of Ireland it is pronounced *gail-ick*.

Gaelic mafia a perceived coterie that favours its own within the **Gaelic** community, particularly within the media in Scotland.

gallus flashy self-confidence; mischievously bold, impish. It has a rogu-ish connotation as its root is in the word 'gallows'. See also **galluses**.

galluses braces, trouser suspenders; a blackly humorous reference to the gallows where convicted criminals would be hanged by their necks.

galsach intae 1. scoff, eat with relish or greed; 2. (old Scots) jaundice. In 'The **Flyting** of Dunbar and Kennedy', one of the earli-est poems to be printed by Scotland's first publishers Chepman and Myllar in Edinburgh in 1507, William Dunbar says that his rival has the flux: 'Thy **gulsoch** gane dois on thy bak it bind' ['Your jaundiced face proves it'].

gangrel beggar, tramp.
　　'I'm nocht but a peer wand'rin' **gangrel**.'
　　George P. Dunbar, *A Whiff o' the Doric*, 1922

gant 1. yawn; 2. with a wide open mouth, often to beg beseechingly; 3. the gannet (*Sula bassana*).

gantry the display of a range of bottled spirits ready to be dispensed behind a bar.

Garde Ecossaise Scots Guard of King Charles VII of France, formed in 1418. See also **Auld Alliance**.

gardyloo (French, *gardez (vous de) l'eau*, 'beware of the water') a warning shout from a **tenement** window in old Scottish towns (one hopes) before the contents of a **chanty** is emptied.

gathering a **gathering** of the **clans** would be a great coming together of Highlanders but in modern usage a social gathering of any size, similar to the original use of **ceilidh**.

gauger   exciseman, government official.
> *The **Gauger** of Dalmore lives again*
> *in verses. An old song*
> *makes history alive again.*
> Norman MacCaig, 'A Man in Assynt', 1968

gaun yersel   literally, 'go on yourself'; a phrase or shout of support for or delight at an endeavour about to completed. A sportsperson, a certainty to score or win, will be encouraged with excited pleasure to **gaun yersel!**

gawkit   stupid, oafish, unpractised in the ways of the world. The **cornkister** 'The **Muckle Gawkit** Gype' describes the foolish antics of a big awkward, open-mouthed laddie from the North East who is unlucky in love.

Gay Gordons   Scottish country dance.
> *Who's for the Gathering, who's for the Fair?*
> *(Gay goes the Gordon to a fight)*
> *The bravest of the brave are at deadlock there,*
> *(Highlanders! march! by the right!)*
> Sir Henry Newbolt, 'The Gay Gordons', 1897

geg/geggie   the mouth, especially in its speech-forming function: 'Shut yer **geggie**!'

gey/giy/gay   very.
> 'Here's tae us, wha's like us? **Gey** few . . . an' they're a' **deid**.'
> Traditional toast

ghillie (Gaelic, *gillie*)   servant; since the destruction of the **clan** system, a gamekeeper. Before that the term ranged from the carrier of the **clan** chief's armour to the farm servant boy.

gies a haun   literally, 'give us a hand'; a request for help or assistance. See also **hauners**.

ginger [*jin-jer* or *ging-er*] 1. a semi-insulting name for a red-haired person (usually denoting Celtic origin) but some redheads are 'proud to be a **ginger**'; 2. [*jin-jer*] a carbonated sugary drink: 'Goannie get us a boatle o' **ginger** frae the chippy?' ['When at the fish bar could you purchase some lemonade on my behalf?']

girdle/griddle simple, round, heavy metal plate for cooking **oatcakes**, scotch **pancakes** and **scones**.

glack yer mitten to drop a coin into someone's hand; hence, to bribe or tip. A **glack** is a valley or hollow.

glaikit stupidly unaware, uncomprehending, backward: 'Don't just stand there looking **glaikit**, **gies a haun**.'

glamour/glamer/glawmir 1. make a noise, commotion; 2. witch-craft, to cast a spell, enchant.

> *Than come зour king and sum lords with ane **glamer**, And reft*
> *him from hir.*

From 1570, describing the abduction and then murder of Mary, Queen of Scots' secretary, Riccio, in *Satirical Poems of the Time of the Reformation*

Glasgow kiss a headbutt. See also **heid**.

gleg (Old Norse, *gleggr*, 'clever') sharp, perceptive, focused (the opposite of **glaikit**).

Glencoe as well as being a physical place, this is shorthand for the massacre of Glencoe in 1692, a shocking event that stands out even in Scotland's bloody history. The government-sanctioned slaughter of men, women and children by troops who had first enjoyed their victims' hospitality broke a Highland taboo.

Glengarry   flat-sided military hat popularised by Raeburn's portrait of MacDonnell of Glengarry in 1822. Similar to a forage cap, it is usually black with a band of red-and-white checked pattern along each side, with two ribbons at the back.

glengore (French, *grand gorre*, 'great pox')   syphilis.

gloamin'   twilight.
> *Roamin' in the **gloamin'** on the **bonnie** banks o' Clyde,*
> *Roamin' in the **gloamin'** wi' ma **lassie** by ma side,*
> *When the sun has gone to rest, that's the time that I like best,*
> *O, it's lovely roamin' in the **gloamin'**!*
Harry Lauder, 'Roamin' in the Gloamin'', 1911

golf/gowf/gauff, etc.   a game played outdoors by hitting a ball into a hole using a club or clubs. Popular worldwide, its modern origins lie in Scotland in the late Middle Ages. A 1457 Act of Parliament under James II is the earliest written example, banning the game so as not to distract men from military training: 'At the **futbal** ande the **golf** be vtterly cryt done and nocht vsyt' ['Football and golf be utterly cried down and not used']. The **links** at St Andrews in Fife are said to be 'the home of golf'.

gowan   daisy.
> *The feildis ouerflouis*
> *With **gouans** that grouis.*
Alexander Montgomerie, 'The Night is Neir Gone', sixteenth century

gowk   1. cuckoo; 2. a fool: On 1 of April you may play **huntegowk**, meaning fool's errand; literally, 'hunt the cuckoo'. See also **preen tail**.
> *Half doun the hill, whaur fa's the linn*
> *Far frae the flaught o' fowk,*
> *I saw upon a lanely whin*
> *A lanely singin' gowk:*
William Soutar (1898–1943), 'The Gowk'

gowk storm   sudden unseasonal weather, either snowfall on a fine spring day or a downpour of heavy rain, usually with thunder and lightning, in summer. Also, the title of a classic 1933 novel by Nancy Brysson Morrison.

gowk's meat   wood sorrel (*Oxalis acetosella*). Comes into flower as cuckoos return in spring.

gowkispintil   lords and ladies flower (*Arum maculatum*); literally, 'cuckoo's penis'.

gowp   beat, throb: 'Ma **heid**'s pure **gowpin**'.'

gowpen/gowpin   cupped hands to form a bowl: 'There's gold in **gowpins**!'

Graham, see **Munro**.

graith (Old Norse, *greithr*, 'make ready', 'prepare')   the kit, tools or equipment needed to carry out a task.

gralloch (Gaelic, *greallach*)   1. (noun) intestines; 2. (verb) to disembowel a deer after the hunt.
> 'There lay the dead stag [with] . . . the miscreant calmly
> proceeding to the **gralloch**.'
> John Buchan, *John Macnab*, 1925

grannie   1. female grandparent (who cannot be pushed or shoved from public road transportation, see **cannae**); 2. rotating steel cowl on top of a **lum**.

Grannie Scotland   personification of Scotland based on the outline of the mainland looking like a nineteenth-century bonneted old woman with a **creel** on her back.

greet   cry. A '**greetin**' face' is an unhappy demeanour, revealing an underlying misery: 'Whit's wrang wi your **greetin**' face?'

Ally bally, ally bally bee,
Sittin' on yer mammy's knee
Greetin' *for a wee* **bawbee,**
Tae buy some Coulter's candy'
Robert Coltart, 'Coulter's Candy', *c.* 1845

Gretna Green   village in the south-west of Scotland just over the border from England. Associated with romance because marriage laws are different between the two countries, so English couples without parental approval to marry would elope and tie the knot at Gretna, sometimes in the blacksmith's forge, the smith striking his anvil symbolising forging the two in wedlock.

grue   to shudder or shiver with cold or fear.

gub   1. punch (in the mouth); 2. resoundingly beat (implying the silencing of an opponent in an overwhelming victory): 'Partick Thistle totally **gubbed** Celtic 4–1 to win the cup.'

guddle   1. a mess: 'My, yer in a right **guddle** there'; 2. to fish using only the hands: 'to **guddle** for trout'.

guid   good: '**Guid** gear gangs in a sma' book' ('Good things come in small packages').

guiser   someone in fancy dress. A child going round doors at Hallowe'en is **guising**. In Shetland the leader of the annual midwinter festival of **Up-Helly-Aa** is called the **Guiser-Jarl** (it is not clear if a new Scots word will be created when a woman finally assumes the post).

gumption   good or common sense.
> ... 'Tis sma Presumption
> To say they're but unlearned clarks,
> And want the **Gumption**.

William Hamilton to Allan Ramsay, 1719

gushe   triangle of land between properties, fields or roads, for example, **Gushetfaulds** in Glasgow.

guttered   very, very drunk. So drunk that you collapse into the gutter – both physically and morally: 'You were totally **guttered** last night, it's a' o'er Facebook!'

guttie   sandshoe or plimsoll.

gyre   a supernatural being, sometimes a witch, sometimes a boy, or at other times a giant.

H

hieland coo

haar   east coast sea mist.

> *The kintra sleeps in* **haar** *frae morn till nicht;*
> *An, gin the sun* **keeks** *throwe, 'tis wi a face*
> *Blae,* **peely-wally** *roon, as tho meenlicht,*
> *Her traivels feenished o her nichtly race.*
> Sheena Blackhall, 'November: A Scots owersett o a Poem bi John
> Clare', 2010

hack   a narrow but deep cut on the hands of a manual worker.

hackit   ugly.

> "'In the name o' the wee man!" bawled the faither, gawpin intae
> the wee mirror. "Whit's happened tae me! Ah look **hackit**! Ah
> look jist like you but aw wrang!"'
> Roald Dahl, *Matilda in Scots*, translated by Anne Donovan, 2019

hackle   feather in a Scotch **bunnet** or **tammy** (see **Tam o'Shanter**), usually military.

haggis   Scotland's national dish is a meaty pudding made from the
minced innards of a sheep combined with oatmeal and suet, seasoned
with pepper, then boiled or roasted in a sheep's stomach . . . delicious.
An integral part of any **Burns Supper**.

hain (Old Norse, *hegna*, 'protect')   hang onto something just in case,
hedge your bets.

ha'in'   having: 'Got any tampons? I'm **ha'in'** the painters in.'

hairy   prostitute (also **hoor**). Mary Magdalene, reformed prostitute
who followed Christ, reputedly covered her 'shame' with her long hair.

hairy bummer   wild bee (*Bombus muscorum*).

hairy woobit   woolly bear caterpillar (*Pyrrharctia Isabella*).

haiver, see **haver**.

hamefare the celebration of a bride's move into the marital home in the Northern Isles. See also **infar cake**.

hameldaeme a holiday at home (usually brought about by lack of funds to do anything else).

hamesucken criminal offence of entering a person's home and assaulting them.

Hampden Park Glasgow Stadium, 'the home of Scottish football', where most international and cup final matches are played. Record crowd attendance was 149,000 for Scotland v. England match in 1937.

handless clumsy, fumble; key quality required by Scottish **fitba** goalies.

handsel a gift or the act of giving a present at the start of a new venture, usually when moving to a new home.

harl/harling roughcast covering on an exterior wall for protection and insulation.

Harry Wraggs Scottish rhyming slang for Partick Thistle football club, based on their nickname the **Jags**. Wragg was a popular mid-twentieth-century racehorse jockey.

haud hold, wait: '**Haud** oan a wee minute, Jimmy.' '**Haud** yer wheesht!'

hauf an' a hauf a measure of whisky and a half pint of beer. See also **chaser**.

haugh alluvial land by a river; for example, North **Haugh**, St.Andrews; **Haugh** of Urr, Dumfries and Galloway.

hauners   help, or a cry for help while being assailed.

haver/haiver   ramble, talk nonsense. The Proclaimers were happy to haver for 500 miles.

> 'Dinna deave [bother] the gentleman w' your **havers**.'
> Sir Walter Scott, *Redgauntlet*, 1824

haw   an exclamation to attract attention: '**Haw**, gie's **hauners!**'

Hawick ball   black-and-white-striped boiled confectionery.

Heart of Midlothian   the site of the old Edinburgh tolbooth and gaol marked on the cobbles outside St Giles' High Kirk. Some people still spit on it as sign of their disdain for authority (and public health) and not as a commentary on Sir Walter Scott's eponymous novel, although perhaps on the Edinburgh **fitba** club of the same name (see **Jambos**).

heather   common heather or ling (*Calluna vulgaris*). Hills purpled by heather are an iconic image of Scotland. You might seek good fortune with a sprig of the rarer 'lucky white heather', especially at a wedding.

heavy   a beer with a higher than normal alcohol content. Often served in a small glass – a wee heavy – to compensate for the strength. See also **export**.

hech and how   the same old routine.

> *What need ye **hech and how**, ladies?*
> *What need ye how for me?*
> *Ye never saw grace at a graceless face,*
> *Queen Mary has nane to gie.*
> Traditional, 'Ballad of Mary Hamilton'

heedrum-hodrum   dismissive Lowland parody of Highland traditional mouth music. See also **heuchter-teuchter**.

hee-haw   nothing: 'Win onything at the bingo?' '**Hee-haw**.'

heid   head; **the heid** or **heidy** is the headteacher or principal. To **stick the heid** on someone is to headbutt them; see **Glasgow kiss**.

heidbanger   nutter.

hem/hames/haimes and brechom   collar for a working horse.
> *A pair of **haimes and brechom** fine,*
> *And without bitts a bridle-renzie.*

From 'Rob's Jock (A very auld Ballat)', in Allan Ramsay, *Tea Time Miscellany*, 1733

heugh   steep cliff or precipice; for example, Clachan Heughs, Dumfries and Galloway; Ravenheugh Sands, East Lothian.

heuchter-teuchter   disparaging term concerning Highland music, implying it has no merit, and is all just emotional shouts and simplistic melodies. See also **heedrum-hodrum** and **teuchter**.

Hibee   supporter of Hibernian Football Club. An Edinburgh derby match will see the **Hibees** play the **Jambos**.

hielan'   concerning or carried out in a Highland manner, the implication being that it is done in an unconventional or obtuse way with an element of *mañana*.

hieland coo   Highland cow (*Bos Taurus*). Highland cattle, though always portrayed as red, come in a variety of colours. Their frightening appearance and long horns belie the gentle nature of an animal used to human companionship through the **droving** tradition.

high doh   if you are 'up to **high doh**', you are extremely worried or anxious.

high heid yin   person in position of authority.

High Road   in the popular song 'The Bonnie Banks of Loch Lomond', a **Jacobite** prisoner in a condemned cell over **the Border** declares that although his friend will live (take the **High Road**) and he will die (take the Low Road), his spirit will return to Scotland first – though he laments that he'll never again meet his true love by the **loch's bonnie** banks.

Highland fling   solo dance said to originate as a test of the agility, balance and stamina of warriors in front of **clan chiefs**. Men had to dance with upraised arms, it is said in imitation of a stag's antlers (see **caber-feidh**), on a small round shield called a 'targe'. Now a popular event at **Highland Games**.

  'I hope I shall not return without having got the **Highland fling**.'
  John Keats, *Letters*, 1818

Highland Games   annual summer celebration in glens, villages, towns and cities across Scotland and the Scottish diaspora of things supposedly **heilan'**. Traditional Scottish heavy sports such as **tossing the caber**, throwing the hammer, and heavy drinking are combined with the lightweight arts of the **Highland fling** and poor-quality local craftworks. Much patronised by members of the Royal Family and moneyed incomers, often feasts of **tartanry**.

Highland Line   border between the Highlands and the Lowlands, which roughly follows the geological Highland fault line from the Firth of Clyde in the west to the Aberdeenshire coast in the east. The Highlands consists of the northern and western mountainous area of Scotland, often penetrated by long sea **lochs**, more heavily influenced by Celtic and Norse culture. The Lowlands are the central and southern areas of Scotland, which are more agricultural and industrial.

hine   haven, harbour, shelter.

hin-end   rear end, backside: 'Get **aff** yir **hin-end** an help yir old maw.'

hing   a modern way of expressing a trend on social media, or an emotion or thing: '**Ken**? It's just a **hing**?'

hingin'   1. rotten, rancid, nasty; 2. hanging: 'He's **hingin'** ontae the beef.' ['He is overweight.']

hippit   suffering pain in the lower back and limbs. Formerly an affliction of agricultural workers, then of factory workers.
'This time the morn's night, **Quean**, **ilka** bone in your body
will be **hippit**, after a day at the mill!'
Jessie Kesson, *The White Bird Passes*, 1958

hirple   walk with a limp.
This is a true talking that Thomas of tells,
*That the hare shall **hirple** on the hard stone*
In the hope of Grace, but Grace gets she none.
The Prophecies of Thomas Rymer, c. 1620, from an older
thirteenth-century tradition

hoatchin'   seething, swarming.
'I hear the rigs are **hoaching** with dope.'
Ian Rankin, *Black and Blue*, 1997

Hogmanay   New Year's Eve; see also **Ne'er Day**. The origins of the word are obscure, maybe French, Gaelic or Norse, possibly meaning 'Holy Month'. The first written record appears in Elgin, Moray, in 1604 as '**hagmonay**'.

holm   small island: in the sea in the Northern Isles, usually used for grazing sheep; by a river or on a flood plain in the Lowlands.

honest men and bonie lasses   people from the town of Ayr, who owe the epithet to Burns.
Auld Ayr, wham ne'er a town surpasses.
For honest men and bonie lasses.
Robert Burns, 'Tam o'Shanter', 1790

honk   vomit (noun) or to vomit (verb); **honkin'** is sick-inducing.

hoodie   hooded or carion crow (*Corvus cornix*). North and west of Inverness **hoodies** have a browner colouring that those further south, which are black and grey.

hoolet, howlat   owl or owlet (*Strigiformes*). 'The Book of the Howlat' is a 1440s poem by Richard Holland. Believing himself ugly, a young owl decides to speak to the most handsome bird of all, the peacock.

hoor   whore. See also **hairy**. A **hoormaister** is a pimp.

hoot   exclamation. Also '**hoots**, mon!', a nickname given to the *Scotsman* newspaper.

> '**Hoot**, Johnnie Rousseau man, what for hae ye sae mony
> **figmagairies**.'
> James Boswell, *Boswell and the Grand Tour*, 1764

horny-golach   earwig (*Dermaptera*); a 'golach' is a beetle. Also known as a 'forkie'.

houghmagandie   sexual intercourse.

> *Whereas our fiscal, by petition,*
> *Informs us there is strong suspicion*
> *That Coachman Dow and Clockie Brown,*
> *Baith residenters in this toun –*
> *In ither words, you, Jock and Sandy,*
> *Hae been at warks o'* **houghmagandie***;*
> *And noo when facts are brought tae light,*
> *Thae facts ye baith deny outright.*
> Robert Burns, 'The Court of Equity', 1786

howff   meeting place, usually a bar or inn. In Dundee the old cemetery is known as the **howff**, where the town's trades once gathered and where old friends will, inevitably, meet.

howtowdie   a big hen bred for the pot.

Hugh, see **Munro**.

hunner   a considerable amount; literally, 'hundreds'.

hurdies   buttocks.
> 'Of hir **hurdies** sche had na hauld.'
> Sir David Lindsay, *Ane Satyre of the Thrie Estaitis, c.* 1552

hydro   1. the North of Scotland Hydro-Electric Board, which oversaw the development of generating electricity from Scotland's lochs and rivers in the period following the Second World War; 2. any such scheme that brought power from the glens. 'Hydro boys' are the engineers and navvies who dug the tunnels and built the dams for **hydro** schemes. The diggers were known as 'tunnel tigers'.

I

inkie-pinkie

ilk/ilka   every.

> *I've heard the lilting, at the **yowe**-milking,*
> *Lasses a-lilting before dawn o' day;*
> *But now they are moaning on **ilka** green loaning;*
> *The Flowers of the Forest are a' wede away.*
>
> Jean Elliot, 'The Flowers of the Forest', 1776

ilk, of that   of the same, usually added to a clan or laird's title, for example, Iain Moncrieffe **of that Ilk** for Iain Moncrieffe of Moncrieffe.

immortal memory, the   a toast to the bard made at every **Burns Supper**.

imphm   an intonation more than a word, which, as the poem opening the introduction says, means 'anything you like'.

> '"**Imphm; imphm; imphm**; there might be something in that!"
> nodding his head and stroking his moustache, as he uttered
> each meditative "**imphm**".'
>
> George Douglas Brown, *The House with the Green Shutters*, 1901

inch/insch   low-lying land near a loch or river, sometimes becoming an island at high tide.

Indyref   the 2014 independence referendum. Also, **Indyref2**, the proposed second independence referendum, date uncertain.

infar cake   a wedding cake made by the bridegroom to welcome a new bride to the matrimonial home; it is broken over her head (not a portent of things to come, it is to be hoped) and distributed to guests. The custom is of Roman origin. See also **hamefare**.

ingin   Dundonian for onion. French onion-sellers were known as 'ingin Johnnies'; after arriving in a ship carrying a cargo of onions, they would disperse from the port of Leith by bicycle and sell their **ingins** all over Scotland. Such trade has a long tradition, with seventeenth-century

Dundee harbour records frequently listing 'Barrels of onyoneis' or 'ingeounis' being landed from the Continent. See also **bridies**.

inkie-pinkie   weak beer.

interdict   a banning order issued by a Scottish court to protect another's rights; for example, a temporary reporting ban being imposed on the media by an interim **interdict**.

intimmers   the interior workings of something, usually mechanical, or even of someone.

Inversneckie   nickname for Inverness, also sometimes Snecky or the Sneck. The Laird of Inversnecky was a comic persona of the Aberdonian music-hall comedian Harry Gordon (1893–1957). Although his character was sketched from Banchory, the same late-Victorian small-town observations rang true of the Highland capital.

Irn Bru [*I-run-broo*]   popular soft drink of tangerine hue 'made in Scotland from girders' with supposed hangover-cure properties. It is able to boast of being Scotland's 'other national drink'; others would argue, quite legitimately, its precedence over whisky.

isnae   is not. 'Aye, it is.' 'Isnae.'

ither   other.
> *O wad some Power the giftie gie us*
> *To see oursels as **ithers** see us!*
> Robert Burns, 'To a Louse (On Seeing One on a Lady's Bonnet, at Church)', 1786

jags

Jacobite supporter of the restoration of the Stewart/Stuart monarchy, primarily in the late seventeenth and eighteenth centuries. The name comes from the Latin for the deposed King James VII of Scotland/II of England and Ireland, and his son James. See also **the king over the water** and **velvet-coated gentleman**.

jags thistle. Also the nickname given to any team with 'Thistle' in its title, primarily Partick Thistle Football Club. Inverness Caledonian Thistle are known as the 'Caley **Jags**'.

jakie (slang) an alcoholic tramp or beggar.

jalouse intuit, work out, suspect.
> 'As you might **jalouse**, I would support the former theory
> [that emigrant Scots influenced the U.S. Declaration of
> Independence], citing the presence at its drafting of a major
> Scottish thinker in John Witherspoon . . .'
> Billy Kay, *The Scottish World: A Journey into the Scottish Diaspora*,
> 2008

Jambos nickname for the Heart of Midlothian Football Club. Founded by members of an Edinburgh dancing club, which was named after Sir Walter Scott's novel. 'The Jambos' comes from rhyming slang for 'hearts' – 'jam tarts'. Currently going through a sticky patch; they were last champions in the 1959–60 season. See also **Hibee**.

jannie school janitor: 'Snomajoabtae was the name we gave our **jannie** – he always said, "It's no ma job tae [do that]."'

jaup to splash. To '**jaup** the water' is to aimlessly waste time or effort.

jaw wave, ripples, aftershock.

Jeddart snails   toffee-flavoured boiled sweets from the Borders town of Jedburgh. More palatable than **Jeddart justice**, where a person was hanged first and questions were asked afterwards.

jeely   jam with a high sugar and low fruit content, placing it at the cheaper end of the market. A **jeely piece** is a jam sandwich.

> 'Kirstie had decoyed him to her room and given him "a jeely-piece".'

Robert Louis Stevenson, *Weir of Hermiston*, 1896

jessie   insulting and derogatory name for a faint-hearted or effeminate boy or man: 'Away, ya big **jessie**.'

Jim/Jimmy   ubiquitous epithet when addressing a male stranger: 'Haw, **Jimmy**! That yir **jeely piece** oan the ground?'

jings   knowingly outdated expression of surprise. Along with other phrases such as 'crivens' and 'help ma' boab', its use has immediate connotations of **The Broons** and Oor Wullie.

jinky   ability to weave and duck, nimble. Jimmy Johnstone, the talented Celtic footballer, was known as '**Jinky**'.

jobby   excrement. Almost impossible to say without bringing the pronounciation of the Glaswegian comedian Billy Connolly to mind: *jaw-bay*. His 1970s story of the **Jobby weecha** is an ode to the cycle of life. Also known as 'keech' and 'toalie'.

Jock   1. an epithet for Scots, used by non-Scots. It often has a derisory tone that many Scots find insulting. Attempts have been made to have its use banned as racist. Best avoided; 2. a Scottish soldier.

Jock Tamson's bairns   egalitarian phrase meaning everyone is human and are all born equal; literally, 'John Thomson's children'. (Jock Tamson is also a term for a penis.) See Burns' poem 'A Man's a Man for a' That.'

jockey   literally, 'wee Jock'; hence a small, lightweight rider, ideal for horseracing.

jooks   fists: 'C'mon, pit up yir **jooks**.'

jotters   be made redundant, get the sack: 'The **jannie**'s got his **jotters** – refused tae clean the **jobby** weecha!'

jouk   duck or dodge out of the way: '**Jouk** an let the **jaw** gae by.' **Joukie** is slippery, elusive.

Joukiedaidles, Wee   the exhausting, exasperating toddler who never gives you a minute's peace but whom you love dearly. From the mid-nineteenth-century poem by James Smith.

juice   carbonated soft drink. See also **ginger** and **skoosh**.

jungle, the   a stand at Parkhead, home stadium of Glasgow's Celtic Football Club, where its most fanatical fans congregate. **Jungle Jims** is rhyming slang for 'Tims', Roman Catholics of Irish origin who founded the club.

Juniors   applies to the lower, non-professional level of Scottish football rather than the age of the players.

Juteopolis   nineteenth-century name for Dundee, which was then the centre of the jute trade. See also **kettle-biler**.

K

kellas cat

kail   curly kale or leaf cabbage (*Brassica oleracea acephala*). To 'scald your lips on other folk's **kail**' is to stick your nose into their business.

kail jockey   hedge sparrow (*Prunella modularis*).

kailyard   reference to late-nineteenth-century artistic interest in the 'simple' life of the rural poor, a lifestyle viewed with rose-tinted longing once it was fast disappearing.

keek   look, peak. If caught taking a **keek**, you could end up with a **keeker**.

keeker   a black eye. Possibly the result of putting up of one's **jooks**.

keelie   fellow, chap, especially from Glasgow – a Glesga **keelie**.

kellas cat   a black variant of the Scottish wildcat, often associated with witches and the appearance of which foretold ill-luck.

kelpie   folkloric water horse, celebrated in huge metal sculptures by Andy Scott erected in 2013 outside Falkirk.

ken   know; often added at the end of a sentence or after a statement for reassurance, **ken**?

kenspeckle   well known, recognised, famous. **Kenspeckle** Grouse is a character in the 'Skulduggery Pleasant' series of books by Derek Landy. See also **sculduddery**.

kent   known. See also **weel-kent**.

kettle-biler   a Dundonian husband who **bides** at home while his wife goes out to work. Female employment in the city's Victorian and early-twentieth-century jute mills was high – women could be paid less

than men for doing the same job (not much has changed, then). See also
Juteopolis.

kiggle-kaggle   in **curling**, to cast a stone so it zigzags off others.
'His lordship has, in delivering the stone, "kettled" it, that is,
imparted to it the motion known as the "**kiggle-kaggle**".'
J. G. Grant, *The Complete Curler*, 1914

kilt   national dress of Scotland. A skirt-like garment made of **tartan**
worn with only the adornment of a pin by women but with various
accoutrements, mainly devised in the nineteenth century, by men:
sporran, **sgian dhu**, etc. Most Scots don *the* **kilt** rarely or only for for-
mal occasions such as weddings. However, it is often the daily dress of
those in Scotland's low-paid tourist service industries, of soldiers, and
by those at the other end of the social scale hoping to express their
Scottishness. See also **filibeg**, **filimore** and **plaid**.

king over the water, the   James III, the exiled **Jacobite** monarchs.
Originally the deposed James VII of Scotland and II of Great Britain
and then his son, the uncrowned James VIII and III (also known as the
Old Pretender), father of Charles (Bonnie Prince Charlie or the Young
Pretender). When toasting their leader thus, Jacobites would pass their
wine or whisky over a glass of water. See also **velvet-coated gentleman**.

kinrick   kingdom. The Unitit **Kinrick** o Great Breetain an Northern
Ireland is the UK in modern Scots.

kirk   church. *The* **Kirk** is specifically the protestant Church of
Scotland. The **Kirk session** is the committee of **elders**.
*The **wee Kirk**, the **Free Kirk***
*The **Kirk** withoot the steeple,*
*The auld **Kirk**, the cauld **Kirk***
*The **Kirk** withoot the people.*
Traditional

kirking   ceremonial attendance at church, usually part of a civic body's inauguration; for example, **kirking** the council.

kiss-ma-luff   hand-kisser, creep.

kist   chest, safe, storage box, coffin. A **kist o' whistles** is a pipe organ.

Klondyker   originally, a name for sending fresh as opposed to pre-served fish to markets abroad in fast steamships, latterly for a Russian fish-factory ship that during the Soviet era would process catches off the coast of Scotland, especially on the north-west coast where road transport could be slow.

knappit knees   knock knees.

kythin'   showing, appearance
   Thou gracious to the gracious art,
   to upright men upright:
   *Pure to the pure, froward thou **kyth'st***
   unto the froward wight.
   Psalm 18: 25–6

L

links

lad o' parts   multi-talented individual or someone with many strings to their bow.

laddie   boy (of any age).
  'Scotty: (*to the waiter*) **Laddie**, I was drinking Scotch a hundred
  years before you were born. And I can tell you that whatever
  this is, it is definitely not Scotch.'
  Star Trek: The Next Generation, 'Relics', 1992

Lady (or Lord) Provost   formerly the head of municipal government; now a more ceremonial post in local councils. It used to be the tradition that a streetlight bearing the city or burgh coat of arms would be stationed outside their home and known as a Provost lamp.

laich   low-lying water-logged ground. The only 'lake' in Scotland is the Lake of Menteith, believed to be a corruption of **laich**.

laird   landowner.
  Wha the de'il hae we gotten for a king,
  *But a wee, wee German **Lairdie** ...*
  Auld Scotland, thou'rt ower cauld a hole,
  For nursin' siccan vermin;
  But the very dogs in England's court,
  They bark an' howl in German ...
  Jacobite song, eighteenth century

laldie   to approach a task with vigorous, muscular enthusiasm: 'Gie it **laldie**!'

lallans   language of the Lowland (Lallan) Scots.

lament   dirge for the dead in music, song or verse.
  I that in heill wes and gladnes
  Am trublit now with gret seiknes

> *And feblit with infermite;*
> *Timor mortis conturbat me.*
> [I that in health was and gladness,
> Am troubled now with great sickness,
> And enfeebled with infirmity;
> Fear of death troubles me.]
> William Dunbar, '**Lament** for the **Makaris**', early sixteenth century

Lammas, see **quarter days**.

land o' the leal   heaven; literally, 'land of the loyal'.

land of the mountain and the flood   Scotland, as described by Sir Walter Scott and later set to music by Hamish MacCunn.
> *O **Caledonia**! stern and wild,*
> *Meet nurse for a poetic child!*
> *Land of the heath and shaggy wood,*
> *Land of the mountain and the flood.*
> Sir Walter Scott, *Lay of the Last Minstrel*, 1805

lang   long. Kirkcaldy, with its main street stretching for nearly a mile, is 'the **lang** toun'; 'lang day' is the Day of Judgement; 'lang Sandy' is a heron; 'lang-luggit' means big-eared , i.e. an eavesdropper; and 'lang-whang' is a long strip of leather or bootlace, hence also the nickname of the twisting 75-mile road from Edinburgh to Ayr via Lanark.

laroch   the stone remains of a homestead or **shieling** in the Highlands.

lassie   girl.
> '"But I will need to know the **lassie's** name first." A name I hadn't spoken aloud in more than a decade. I thought of her name every day, a hundred times or more . . .'
> Anna Durand, *Gift-Wrapped in a Kilt*, 2018

laverock   skylark (*Alauda arvensis*).

lazy bed a traditional **crofting** method of agriculture where raised mounds of earth and/or sand are mixed with manure and used to grow crops in the poor soils of the Highlands and Islands. Potatoes grow well in **lazy beds**, hence the devastation caused by the potato blight in the Great Highland Famine of the mid-nineteenth century.

leal/leyil loyal.
> 'To be cuming **leyill** and trewe men and seruandis to the
> forsayd Sir Johne Campbell.'
> *The Book of the Thanes of Cawdor, 1236–1742*

lea-rig unploughed strip of grassland, usually a field left fallow as part of crop rotation.
> *Will ye gang o'er the **lee rig**,*
> *My ain kind dearie, O;*
> *And cuddle there fu' kindly,*
> *Wi' me, my kind dearie, O!*
> Robert Fergusson, 'The Lee Rig', 1776

leid language: the 'Dictionar o the Scots **Leid**' ('Dictionary of the Scots Language') records its earliest use around 1380, in the poem 'Legends of the Saints' by John Barbour (1316–1395).

lek, see **capercailzie**.

licht light. The red light that guided returning fishing boats back to Arbroath Harbour is the source of the nickname of the town's football team, the Red Lichties.

lift sky, heavens.
> 'Airlie in the morning, when the **lift** is pure and temperate.'
> Hector Boece, *The History and Chronicles of Scotland*, 1527

lifting day spring day in the Highlands and Islands when cattle, having been indoors all winter, were taken outside again. Sometimes feed had been so scarce during that time that the emaciated animals had to be carried or lifted out.

links   seaside sand dunes, usually referring to a **golf** course on them, such as at St Andrews, Carnoustie or Troon.

lintie   linnet (*Acanthis cannabina*), or small songbird. A person cheerfully singing could be compared to a **lintie**.

Lion Rampant   flag, banner or shield with red beast on a yellow or gold background rearing up on its back legs, facing left and roaring. It has been the royal standard of the Scottish monarch since at least the reign of Alexander II in 1222.

loch   lake. Difficult for non-Scots to pronounce. A 'lochan' is a small lake (and just as tricky to say).

loch-lubbertie   jellyfish.

Lockerbie lick   a slash on the face, the favourite method of wounding among the Johnston clan in the time of the **reivers**.

lockfast   secured place, box or **kist**.
  'Thar was deliverit til Alexander Naper . . . be the auditouris of
  the cheker, vij assais of gold [etc.] . . . in a lokfast box.' (1453)
  The Exchequer Rolls of Scotland, 1264–1600

Lord Provost, see **Lady Provost**.

Lorne sausage   a square of minced beef and pork mixed with rusk and spices, originating in the Lorne area of **Argyll**; popular at breakfast.

loup   loop. A **Grassmarket loup** is the hangman's rope in Edinburgh. See also **galluses**.

loupin'   something that has gone off, smelly or disgusting. See also **mingin'** and **bowffin'**.

Louseland   seventeenth-century derogatory English name for Scotland, the lice in question being known as **Scots Greys**. Some lodging houses were said to be so infested that beds became known as 'scratchers'. See also **meevin'**.

lowp   to jump (on). Outside old inns a **lowpin-on** stane for mounting a **cuddy** might still be found.

lum   chimney: '**Lang** may yir **lum reek**.'

lumber   1. a girl- or boyfriend   2. a date or a pick-up on a night out: 'Ah read this *Scottish Words* book and by using a' the **gallus lallans** it fair helped me get a **lumber** (an' no a **loupin'** yin either)!'

M

malt

Mac/Mc   prefix for Gaelic surname meaning 'son of' though almost universally used for all genders. 'Daughter of' is Nic. Most surnames will have spelling variants and some will be anglicised versions with the 'son' transferred to the end: MacDhòmhnaill, MacDonald, Macdonald, McDonald, Mcdonald, NicDonald, McDonnell, McConnell, Donaldson, Donald.

MacDonald's disease   infection of the chest. Such infections were often caused by poverty and the damp climate of the West Highlands, prevalent in inner cities where members of the clan MacDonald were often exiled. See also **Clearances**.

machair (Gaelic)   pasture land on sand dunes, especially along the western seaboard of the Hebrides and in Galloway. This unique habitat is known for its beautiful wild flowers.

> *I make my circuit*
> *In the fellowship of the saint,*
> *On the **machair**, on the meadow,*
> *On the cold heathery hill.*

Traditional Gaelic Catholic prayer, 'Michael the Victorious', collected by Alexander Carmichael in *Carmina Gadelica*

macintosh   waterproof coat named after Scottish chemist Charles MacIntosh (1766–1843) who invented a method of rubberising fabric.

Maggie wi the mony feet   centipede (*Chilopoda*).

mainland   to a Hebridean islander, the landmass of Scotland, but on the Northern Isles, **Mainland** is the largest island in both the Orkney and Shetland archipelagos.

mains   farm; for example, **Mains** of Gray, Rossmains.

makar   in the past, a maker but now almost exclusively a poet, either one of the late medieval poets – Henryson, Dunbar, Douglas and their circle – or, since 2004, Scotland's laureate poet, known as the **Scots Makar**. See **lament**.

malt   1. a grain, usually barley, that has been dried and germinated as part of whisky-making; 2. the end product, whisky itself. Malt whisky usually refers to a single malt whisky, i.e. one that has not been blended or mixed with other whiskies. See also **usquebaugh**.

mankit/manky   dirty, filthy; see also **bowffin'**.
> 'You **manky** Scots git.'
> Sir Robin, *Monty Python and the Holy Grail*

manse   house provided by a parish for the minister of the **kirk**. A **daughter** (or **son**) **of the manse** is a child of a minister.

marches   the old boundaries of a town or burgh. **Common riding** or **riding the marches** is the annual circumnavigation of these boundaries on horseback, usually combined with a local holiday, in many towns in southern Scotland.

Martinmas, see **quarter days**.

Master   title of a baron's male heir.
> 'A placard was hung above the hutch, bearing these words in something of the following disposition:
>> JAMES DURIE
>> FORMERLY **MASTER** OF BALLANTRAE
>> CLOTHES NEATLY CLOUTED.'
> Robert Louis Stevenson, *The Master of Ballantrae*, 1889

mavis   the song thrush (*Turdus philomelos*); also called a throstle. It features in placenames such as Mavisbank House, Midlothian.

maw   mother. '**Yir maw**' is an ambiguous phrase that can be used as a response, possibly as an insult, to dispute a fact stated: 'These new English whiskies are as good as any single **malt**.' '**Yir maw!**'

mawkit/mockit   filthy, dirty. A **mawk-flee** is old Scots for a bluebottle.

mawsie   1. a big woman of round proportions, motherly but possibly ill-kempt; 2. woollen jumper, possibly from the French heavy fabric *marseille*.

meal mob   urban rioters who protested about shortages of oatmeal created by speculators withholding it from sale to increase prices, such as occurred in Perth in January 1773.

mealy-pudding   savoury sausage made from oatmeal, offal, suet and other ingredients of the cook's choice. Sometimes called a **white pudding** to distinguish it from black pudding, which has blood added to it.

> *All of a sudden a great **mealy puddin'** came flyin' through the air,*
> *It hit fermer Carse like a kick up the a**e and knocked him doon the stairs . . .*
> Traditional rhyme

meer-swine   dolphin or porpoise (*Delphinus*).

meevin'   infested.

> 'I cam hame on leave an flung aff ma claes in the shed afore I gid into the hoose. They were jist **meevin'** wi' lice.'
> Alec Pratt MM, Royal Horse Artillery, First World War

Meg Mullach (Gaelic, *molach*, 'hairy')   Hairy Meg, a small hairy house spirit in the shape of a small girl, said to be a servant to the Grant family of Tullochgorum.

meikle, see **muckle**.

mercat 1. any market; 2. the marriage market. An eligible bachelor or spinster would be described as **mercat-ripe**. To **mak' one's mercat** is to become engaged but to **lose one's mercat** is to fail to make a match.

mercat cross market cross, the centre point of a burgh, where proclamations and punishments were handed out. Many survive, most crowned with a carved unicorn, the ancient symbol of the Scots kingdom, and still the venue for proclamations.

merchant schools fee-paying schools founded by the philanthropical Merchant Company of Edinburgh in the late seventeenth century, originally as charitable hospitals.

merry-begotten an illegitimate child.

Merry Dancers Shetland name for the Northern Lights, the *Aurora borealis*.

messages provisions, or the act of going shopping for daily foodstuffs. When asked if his verses had underlying meaning the poet Norman MacCaig replied ,'If you want a **message**, go to Tesco's.'

mibees maybe. When asked a question he didn't want to answer, the imperious but **canny** Scottish **fitba** player Kenny Dalgleish famously replied, '**Mibees** aye, **mibees** naw.'

michty me exclamation; short for 'Almighty, save me', one of the many ways God-fearing Scots would prevent breaking the Second Commandment: Thou shalt not take the name of the LORD thy God in vain (Exodus 20:7).

midden rubbish, refuse or dung heap. Archaeologically, the source of many historic objects now in the country's museums. Contemporary Scots teenagers would feel culturally deprived if their parents or carers did not regularly shout at them, 'This bedroom is like a **midden**!'

midge/midgie/mudge   tiny wee biting flying insect (*Culicoides impunctatus*), perfectly suited to Scotland's warm, wet, humid summer climate. Individually they are small but swarm in great clouds especially in the Highlands just as the tourist season hits its peak.

'Ye hae fasted lang, and worried on a **midge**.'
Proverb

'There iss nothing that the **mudges** like to see among them better than the English towerist with a **kilt**.'
Neil Munro, *Para Handy*, 1906

mince   minced beef. **Mince** an' tatties is said to be a favourite Scottish dish, though tellingly it is never on the menu in any of the country's restaurants. This is probably because it has been cooked so badly so often at home no one wants to eat it when dining out. In Dundee – a place with a unique gastronomic culture (even for Scotland) – a mince roll is one of the healthy options available in the cafe at the city's hospital. A Dundonian may say I am 'talkin' **mince**'. N.B. **piskies** are too bourgeois to eat mince. See also **tatties**.

mim   prudish. '**Mim** as a May **puddock**' – frogs are said to stay silent from May to autumn.

mingin'   smelly, disgusting, putrid. In Glasgow something exceptionally horrible may be 'pure **mingin**''. See also **bowffin'**.

mink   someone who is **mingin'** or person with **mingin'** or **bowffin'** habits.

mixter-maxter   mixed up, scattered. See also **rach-ma-reesil**.

mochie   1. of weather, close, damp, muggy; 2. mouldy, moth-eaten.

mocket   dirty, soiled.

Mod   annual celebration of Gaelic culture – song, Highland dancing, instrumental music, drama, sport and literature. Competitions for all ages are held, with a gold medal a much valued prize. The venue changes each year. The Royal National Mod has been run by *An Comunn Gàidhealach* for over a century with the aim of preserving and developing the Gaelic language.

mollach (Gaelic, *mallachd*)   curse: '**Mollach** on ye!'

mon   abbreviation of 'come on'. You could invite an opponent to engage in physical combat with '**Mon** aheid, ya **bawbag**!'

Mons Meg   a huge fifteenth-century cannon in Edinburgh Castle.
'A monument of our pride and poverty. The size is immense,
but six smaller guns would have been made at the same expense,
and done six times as much execution as she could have done.'
Sir Walter Scott, 1829

moothie   mouth organ. Cheap, simple to play and fitting in a pocket, the **moothie** and the jew's harp were the instruments of Scotland's poor working people and in the cold of winter did not need dexterous finger movement.

moss troopers   seventeenth-century Border raiders; see **reivers**.

mouth music (Gaelic, *port-a-beul*)   Even cheaper than a **moothie**, with echoes of ancient times, mouth music is the musical score or song sheet of the oral, bardic tradition in which words, or nonsense words, are sung to help remember a tune. An erroneous tradition has it that these originated to keep alive pipe tunes after the **bagpipes** were banned following the 1745 **Jacobite** uprising – but they weren't.

muckle   big, large amount: 'Mony a **puckle** maks a **muckle**' ['Many little things add up to a lot'].

multis   post-Second World War multi-storey housing.

Munro   any one of the 289 Scottish mountains over 3,000 feet high, named after the Victorian mountaineer Sir Hugh Munro, who classified them. Other height classifications for mountains are: Hugh, under 2,000 feet; Donald, at least 2,000 feet; Graham, between 2,000 and 2,499 feet; and Corbett, between 2,500 and 2,999 feet.

Munro-bagger   hillwalker or climber who is in the process of completing or has completed the ascent of all the **Munros**.

murder-polis   a west-coast expression meaning a place is very busy, heaving (as when a large crowd gathers around the scene of a violent crime). See also **polis**.

myresnipe   common snipe (*Gallinago gallinago*). If you 'meet with a **myresnipe**' you are stuck in a bog.

N

neuk

neb   nose: 'Yiv a'ways got tae get yir **neb** in, eh?'

Ne'er Day   New Year's Day. See also **Hogmanay** (Ne'er Day's Eve).

neuk   1. nook or corner, place of shelter. A cosy place by a fire is an **ingle-neuk**; 2. a cove or cliffside harbourage. The **East Neuk** is the collective name for the fishing villages along the Fife coast.

nicky-tams   string or straps tied below the knees to prevent an agricultural worker's **breeks** getting **clartit** with mud.
> *Fin I wis only ten years auld I left the pairish school*
> *Ma faither **fee'd** me tae the **mains** tae airn ma milk an' meal*
> *Well I first pit on ma **nerra breeks** tae hap ma **spin'le trams***
> *Syne I buckl'd roon ma **knappit** knees a pair o' **nicky tams**.*
> Traditional Bothy Ballad, 'Nicky Tams'

nip   a measure of whisky, a **dram**. If you **nip someone's heid** you are nagging or giving them a hard time.
> 'Ma **heid** is fair **nippin'** me,' said Paddy, 'I think ma eardrums are burst.'
> Agnes Owens, *Agnes Owens: The Complete Short Stories*, 2011

nippy sweetie   woman or girl who always has a barbed retort or who will make a sharp observation.

noo, see **enoo**, and the Introduction.

not proven   verdict unique to the Scottish legal system when a jury expresses its belief that the defendant's innocence has not been established but that the prosecution has not sufficiently demonstrated guilt.

numpty   person carrying out a foolish act or proven to have done so: 'Yir doin' ma **heid** in, ya **numpty**.'

nuttata   not at all.

> '**Nuttata** bahthirt.' ['Not at all bothered.']
> Norman Watson, *The Dundee Dicshunury*, 2011

nyaff   insulting term for a diminutive, insignificant person, often small-minded, usually irritating or a **numpty**. See also **shilpit**.

Old Firm

oatcake   staple of the Scottish diet for centuries. Before modern farming methods oats grew better in Scottish conditions than any other cereal crop. Quick and easy to cook, oatmeal is usually mixed with water and butter or fat to form a thin biscuit and cooked on a **girdle** either at home or on the move.

och   multifaceted expression used universally; expressive sound at the beginning of any number of statements: '**Och**, away an' bile yer bum, ya **numpty!**' See also **ach**.

ochone   alas; Highland expression of regret.

> *Ochain, ochain, ochain uiridh*
> *Is goirt mo chridhe, laoigh,*
> *Ochain, ochain, ochain uiridh*
> *Cha chluinn t'athair ar caoidh.*
> [**Ochone, ochone**, my little one,
> my heart is deathly sore,
> **Ochone, ochone**, my little one,
> your father cannot hear.]

Marion Campbell, Mrs MacGregor of Glenstrae (fl. 1570), 'Griogal Cridhe/Lament for MacGregor of Glenstrae'; her husband, the child's father, could not hear because he had been beheaded by her own father, 'Grey Colin' Campbell of Glenlyon.

> ***Quhen** scho, ouircome with siching sair and sad,*
> *With mony cairfull cry and cauld '**Ochone!**'*
> *Now is my breist with stormie stoundis stad.*

Robert Henryson – a Lowlander – 'Testament of Cresseid', *c.* 1500

ocht   anything.

> *Apon him self he tuk full gret trawaill*
> *To fend his men, gyff that mycht **ocht** awaill.*

Blind Harry, *The Wallace, c.* 1480

Old Firm, the   collectively Glasgow's **fitba** establishment, Celtic and Rangers, who between them dominate all other Scottish clubs. Over the years the **Old Firm** have created their own language, including such terms as 'the Shame Game', which describes a 1987 match that saw brawls and **square goes** on the pitch, three players sent off and over sixty supporters arrested. Four players were later charged with 'conduct likely to cause a breach of the peace'. Each team's favourites also often have Scots nicknames indicative of their attributes as player, for example the elusive 'Jinky' Johnstone or the hard-working ball-carrier Willie Henderson, known as 'the Wee Barra'.

on-ding   heavy fall of rain or snow: 'Crivens, there bin a right **on-ding** o' snaw o'er nicht.'

opporchancity   delightful combination word invented by the mid-twentieth-century music-hall comic duo Francie and Josie that gives the impression that the character speaking is the worse for drink.

orra   Glaswegian shortening of 'all the', as in wishing someone farewell with '**orra** best'.

outby   outside, nearby: 'The **cludgie's outby** at the **but an' ben**.'

outlander   foreigner. Also the title of an extremely popular historical romance TV series, based on the books by American Diana Gabaldon, in which a twentieth-century nurse is transported back to eighteenth-century Scotland at the time of the **Jacobite** uprising. Tourists from around the world flock to visit the film locations all over Scotland where real and *Outlander* history mix like some psychedelic **tartan**. See also **sassenach**.

outwith outside, beyond.

> 'Parte of the boundis foirsaidis wirk wyn cary, fyne, refyne and transporte to ony parte of this realme or outwith the samin mineralis and metallis.'
>
> Act anent the Mynes, 1593

owergyaan overcome, overpower.

> *Troy is overgane with girse and wilde scroggis* [gorse and wild bushes]
>
> *The Complaynt of Scotland*, 1549

oxter armpit.

> *Their jaws are chafts, their hands when closed are neives,*
> *Their bread's not cut in slices, but in sheives,*
> *Their armpits are their **oxters**, palms are lufts,*
> *Their men are chields, their timid fools are cuiffs*
>
> Robert Leighton, 'Scotch Words', 1869

P

pot still

Paddy's Milestane   slang name for the Ailsa Craig, a prominent rock in the Firth of Clyde, a recognisable marker to nineteenth-century Irish immigrants, indicating that they were nearing their destination, the city of Glasgow. See also **Ailsa cock**.

pairt   part. A **lad/lass o'pairts** is a boy or girl from a poor background who makes good.

Paisley pattern   elaborate, usually colourful, cloth design inspired by Persian fabrics, especially Kashmir shawls imported during the colonial era and manufactured in the industrial weaving mills of the Scottish town of Paisley. The teardrop motif represents the Zorastrian tree of life.

paldies, see **peever**.

paleerie   tantrum, fit: 'Wid ye look at the big **wean**, ha'in' a **paleerie** when he **disnae** get his ain way.'

pan drop   small, white, hard, mint sweet; favoured by the **kirk**-going classes to **sook** during a long sermon.

pan loaf   slang for talking with an exaggerated Glaswegian upper-middle-class accent; **pan loaf** = 'toaf', i.e. toff.

pancake   a Scotch **pancake** is thick and cooked on a **girdle**; in England it is known as a drop scone.

panel   the accused at a trial.
> 'In 1928, nineteen years after a jury, by a majority of nine to six, found the **panel** guilty as libelled, and Lord Guthrie had assumed the black cap and pronounced sentence of death in the usual form, Oscar Slater's conviction was quashed.'
> Alasdair Alpin MacGregor, *The Golden Lamp*, 1968

partan   crab: 'Yon likes a **dram**, his **neb** is ridder than a **partan**'s tae [claw].' **Partan bree** is crab soup.

patent still   two tanks used to distil grain whisky. See also **pot still** and **usquebaugh**.

patter, the   1. talk, chat, prattle, often associated with Glaswegian slang; 2. in older Scots, to repeat prayers mechanically without true devotion.

pavey   pavement: 'Hey, dude! Whit's happ'nin' oan the **pavey**?'

paw   father. See **The Broons**.

pawky   showing shrewd character, often allied with a dry sense of humour, like the eponymous hero of Galt's *The Provost*.
    'My canny friends came to me; saying, "For God's sake,
    Mr. **Pawkie, tak' tent**."'
    John Galt, *The Provost*, 1822

peasebrose   old-fashioned dish of flour ground from peas mixed with water.

pech   pant, breathe heavily from exertion: 'How are ye gettin' oan tossing the **caber**?' '**Pechin**'!'

peedie   small, **wee**, especially in the Orkney Islands. **Peedie Tatties** are actually delicious cinnamon-coated toffee sweets made by Argos Bakery in Stromness.

peel   fortified tower or house, especially in the Borders.
    '. . . so closely does it resemble a **pele** tower that it might easily
    be mistaken for one.'
    David MacGibbon and Thomas Ross, *The Castellated and Domestic
    Architecture of Scotland from the Twelfth to the Eighteenth Century*, 1892

peely-wally   white, pale: 'First weekend of the **Fair** and **doon the watter** all you can see are **peel-wally** bodies of **Weegies** on the beaches.'

peenge   moan, whine: 'Dinnae **peenge**, it'll soon be Christmas.'

peenie   apron, pinafore.
'She took a terrible notion o' me. If I had a blue **peenie** she must have a blue **peenie** as well.'
Nan Shepherd, *The Weatherhouse*, 1930

pee-the-bed   dandelion.
'Eating these leaves has such a powerful effect on the bladder that the great dandelion name has been usurped by upstart colloquialisms like pissabed and **peethebed**.'
Sally Magnusson, *The Life of Pee*, 2010

peever   the stone or crushed drinks can used in the children's game of hopscotch. The game itself is known as **peevers**. Also known as 'paldies'.

peh   Dundonian for pie. See also **Scotch pie**.
'A **peh**'s a **peh** fur a' that, ispaishully in Dundee.'
David Phillips, 'Pehs', 1966

pelters   going fast: 'Oor Wullie's goin' **pelters** in his **bogie** wi' P.C. Murduch **pechin'** efter him.'

pend   lane or alleyway between two buildings or walls. **The Pend** is the restored medieval gatehouse of Whithorn Priory, owned by the National Trust for Scotland.

petted lip   the bottom lip extended to show childish petulance. A spoilt child denied something might be told, 'Don't give me the **petted lip**.'

petticoat tails   shortbread baked in a circle with a scalloped edge like a petticoat hanging down under a dress, then divided into tail-shaped biscuit triangles.

pewlie Willie   herring gull (*Larus argentatus*).

philibeg, see **filibeg**.

philamore, see **filimore**.

pibroch (Gaelic, *pìobaireachd*)   pipe music. Nowadays it is associated with ceòl mór played on the **bagpipe** (see **ceol beag**) but in the past it could also be associated with that played on the fiddle as well as on the clarsach (a Gaelic harp). See also **urlar**.

> *I have been happy*
> *in this great house,*
>
> *living it up*
> *on the dancefloor,*
>
> *fiddle music*
> *making me sleepy,*
>
> *pibroch*
> *my dawn chorus.*

Màiri nighean Alasdair Ruaidh/Mary McLeod (*c.* 1616–*c.* 1706)
'Tuireadh'/'Blue Song'; English version by Robert Crawford

Pict (Latin, *pictii*, 'the painted')   In his *Agricola* in 98 CE the Roman historian Tacitus uses this term to describe a tribe of Celtic people in **Caledonia** who painted or tattooed themselves. Their power base was in the north and east of Scotland, where many of their beautifully decorated but enigmatic carved stones survive. By the ninth century they had merged with the Gaelic-speaking tribes of Dál-Riata from the west to form the Kingdom of Alba, the prototype Scottish state. 'Pit' is the prefix to a placename indicating **Pictish** origin; for example, Pitlessie, Fife; Pittodrie, Aberdeenshire.

'You gave the peoples – pious teacher – Christ's commands,
long awaited, drawing to yourself the **Pictish** hordes. Revering
idols in death's shadow, they were defiled, but turned to Christ,
his love their guide.'
Anonymous Whithorn monk, 'The Miracles of St. Nynia', *c.* 780

piece   sandwich. A **playpiece** is a schoolchild's mid-morning snack. See
also **jeely**.

pintil   penis.
'He is als good a man as ever pissed with a pintle.'
Fergusson's Scottish Proverbs, 1641

pipes, **the**, see **bagpipes**.

pish   piss. If you are **pished** you are drunk.

piskie   a member of or associated with the **Episcopal Church** of
Scotland.

pit awa'   to pawn.
Gude guide me, are ye hame again, and hae ye got nae wark?
*We've naething **noo** tae **pit awa**, unless your auld blue sark.*
'Factory Girl', pseudonym of Ellen Johnston (*c.* 1835–1873),
'The Last Sark'

plaid/plaidie   length of cloth, sometimes used as a cloak, usually of **tar-tan** material and thus can also sometimes refer to the **kilt** or the **filimore**.

plook   a pus-filled spot, often prominent on a teenager's **neb**. The
'**Plook** on the Plinth' Award is presented each year for the most dismal
town in Scotland.

plouter   play around without purpose: 'Dinnae **plouter** wi yir
porridge!'

pockle/pauckle   pocket or take possession of something, usually illic-itly: 'He'd **pockle** the **bawbees** oot yir **sporran** if he had hauf a chance.'

poind   the sale of household goods to raise funds by a creditor.

poke   bag. A **poke o' chips** is a bag of French fries. In genealogy the last of a line is known as **the shakin's o' the poke**, i.e. the crumbs at the foot of the bag.

pokey-hat   1. triangular three-pointed hat made from folded newspa-per for a child; 2. an ice-cream cone.

polis   the police: 'Whau's at the door, Flora?' 'Oh, Charlie! It's the **polis**.'

port-a-beul, see **mouth music**.

pot still   a copper pot for distilling whisky; the shape of each still is said to influence the taste. See also **patent still** and **usquebaugh**.
   'In Glasgow the whisky aficianado will beat a path to the
   Pot Still, the Bon Accord, or the Ben Nevis, all pubs with a
   fabulous array of whiskies for sale.'
   Rachel McCormack, *Chasing the Dram: Finding the Spirit of Whisky*,
   2017

potato scone, see **tattie scone**.

potted-heid   potted meat from the hough or shin.
   '... **potted heid**, which is common all over Scotland.'
   Margaret Bennett, *Oatmeal and the Catechism: Scottish Gaelic Settlers
   in Quebec*, 2003

poultice   an irritating or annoying person (west).

pow   1. head of a person, animal or object; 2. pool, marsh, also a drainage ditch, man-made channel or pool; such as **Pow** of Airth on the River Forth, home to the Scottish Renaissance navy; **Pow** of Inchaffray.

powsowdie (*pow*, head; *sowdie*, mash)   **mixter-maxter** of foodstuffs. See **sheep's heid**.

precentor   person who leads the singing in a **kirk**, especially in the Free Church (see **Disruption**).

precognition   in law a statement by a witness to establish the facts of a case before a trial begins.

preen   pin. **Preen tail** or **tailie day** is 2 April, when those who were **gowk**-ed had paper tails pinned to their backs or arses.

prent buik   printed book. If you **speir like a prent buik**, you are speaking with assumed assurance that belies little real knowledge.

press   cupboard; one built into the wall is a common feature in Scottish architecture from prehistoric Skara Brae to Victorian **tenements**.

principal   headteacher of a school. A **principal teacher** is the head of a particular department in a school.

Provost, see **Lady** (or **Lord**) **Provost**.

puckle   little, small amount. See also **muckle**.

puddock   frog (*Anura*).
　　*A **puddock** sat by the lochan's brim,*
　　*An' he thocht there was never a **puddock** like him.*
　　John M. Caie, 'The Puddock', 1934

puggled   confounded, perplexed, tired out.

puggy   barrel. In a bar or casino, a one-armed bandit is known as a **puggy machine**. A **belly-huddroun** might be **tee-named 'Puggy'**.

pullashies/puhlashee   a **tenement** washing-line running between upper-storey apartments and (usually) a telephone pole, using a pulley to pay out the line and bring it in again. '**Pillie-schief**: the sheaf or groved roller . . . in a pulley block' (*DSL*).

pure   in the West of Scotland a describer word before a noun, verb or adverb to give emphasis, most famously in actor Elaine C. Smith's catchphrase, '**pure** dead brilliant'.

pursuer   in civil law the party bringing or 'pursuing' an action.

purvey (French, *porveeir*)   the food and drink provided at a wedding or a funeral.

pyot   magpie (*Pica pica*).
   'The schrieching **pyets** daubed a' our barn.'
   The Scots Magazine, June 1745

quaich

quaich   broad shallow cup with handles used for toasts; often presented and engraved as a prize, gift or marking a special event. An early nineteenth-century **quaich** in the collection of the National Museums of Scotland is described in the catalogue as 'two-handled wooden quaich mounted in silver, with a plate inside engraved with Wallace's tree and "Tor Wood 1294", "To the immortal memory of Sir William Wallace"', and another as 'bronze quaich made from the boiler plug of the Tay Bridge disaster locomotive 1878'.

quair   book, for example, *The King's Quair* by King James I (*c.* 1424).

quarter days   the four **quarter** or **term days** in the Scottish calendar, which divide the year into four, loosely based on old Celtic divisions of seasons, when workers would be employed for a set period from the **quarter day**: Candlemas, 2 February; Whitsun, seven Sundays after Easter (usually at the end of May or beginning of June); Lammas, at the beginning of August; and Martinmas, 11 November. New working contracts as well as celebrations would take place at the Lammas fair, which is still a local holiday in towns such as St Andrews.

quean/quine   in the north-east a young, unmarried girl or woman.
> 'Sa monie puir **quynes** cared nocht to fall . . . in . . . fornication becaus they have nothing to pey ane penaltie and so escap.'
> Records of the Kirk Session of Brechin, 1617

quhat   what.
> *Quhat drowsie sleepe doth syle your eyes allace*
> *Ye sacred brethren of Castalian band.*
> King James VI, *c.* 1585

quhen   when, whence.
> *In Scotland fell neire the like cais*
> *Be Fynlaw Makbeth that than was,*
> *Quhen he had murtherist his aune eme*
> *Throu hope at he had of a dreme,*

> *That he saw forow that in sleping,*
> **Quhen** *he wes dwelland with the king,*
> Andrew of Wyntoun, 'Makbeth', *c.* 1420

quhilk   which.

> *For him also I powrit out mony teirs,*
> *First* **quhen** *he maid himself possessor of this body.*
> *Of the* **quhilk** *then he had not the heart.*
> Mary, Queen of Scots, 'Sonnet to Bothwell', anonymous translation
> from the original Latin

quine, see **quean**.

quink goose   brent or greylag goose (*Branta bernicla* or *Anser anser*).

R

rovies

Rab Ha' a greedy person. Robert Hall (d. 1843) was a famous Glasgow glutton. Originally a labourer, he found fame when people began to take bets on how much he could eat. A broadsheet obituary stated that 'those that staked their money on his powers were rarely the losers'.

rach-ma-reesil mixed up. See also **mixter-maxter**.

radge/raj crazy, insanely enthusiastic: 'She's **pure radge**, by the way.'

ragman a document with seals attached; infamously the late-thirteenth-century **ragman rolls**, documents bearing the seals of various Scottish nobles, pledging support for King Edward I of England during the Wars of Independence.

raivel mix up, confuse, become baffled.

ramgunshoch a **crabbit**, ill-tempered, rude individual.

rammy fight, free-for-all. 'Black Friday sales? **Dinnae** gae there, itza **pure rammy**.'

ramstam helter skelter, in an uncoordinated way.

randan a wild night's drinking and partying.

rant a vigorous dance-music tune.
> Sae **rantinly** and sae wantonly, sae dauntinly gaed he
> For he played a tune and he danced aroon, below the gallows tree.
> 'MacPherson's **Rant**', traditional

rashes rushes; given currency by Burns' 'A dance: grein greus ye **rasses**' and first recorded in the Straloch Lute manuscript of 1627–9.

rashie-coat a coat worn by the very poor, woven of rushes, famously by Cinderella in the Scottish version of the tale.

rax   wind up: '**Dinnae rax** yir cackie [excrement]' is an instruction to keep calm.

reamin'   overflowing. In Burns' poem, '**reamin'** swats' of ale are drunk by Tam o'Shanter and Souter Johnnie.

rector   1. headmaster of a school; 2. representative elected by students on a university's council, often a celebrity or a **weel-kent** face.

Red Biddy   very nasty mix of red wine and meths (methylated spirits) drunk by the most impoverished of alcoholics.

red pudding   north-east meat and meal pudding containing smoked pork. See also **mealy-pudding**.

redd   clear out, spring clean, tidy. To **redd one's crap** is to clear your throat (crop), i.e. let it all out.

reek   smell, smoke. During the nineteenth century, Edinburgh gained the nickname '**Auld Reekie**' due to the air pollution from industry and the use of coal from domestic fires. See also **lum**.

reel   a spinning dance, perhaps performed at a **ceilidh**.

reestit mutton   Shetland mutton cured in saltwater for a fortnight, then smoked over a peat fire for a week.

refreshments   euphemism for alcoholic drinks. At a **Highland Games** there will usually be a tent offering '**refreshments**'.

reiver   in the sixteenth and seventeenth centuries, a cross-Border raider. The distinctive helmets of the period gave rise to the **reivers'** nickname, the 'steel bonnets'.

ridder   to blush with embarrassment: 'She has an' aw! Look, she's got a **pure ridder**.'

riding the marches, see **marches**.

rig   strip of agricultural land. See also **lea-rig, runrig**.

rive   tug, pull down. If you '**rive yer faither's bunnet**', you outshine him.

roaring game   curling, because of the sound the stone makes as it rumbles over the ice.

roaster   modern slang for an idiot. A protestor's placard during US President Trump's visit to Scotland read, 'Yir **maw** was an immigrant ya **roaster**.'

rone   the guttering on a roof. The **roan pipe** is the vertical pipe down the side of a building leading water from gutter to drain.

rood   the cross of Christ's crucifixion. **Holyrood** is the site of both the Scottish monarch's palace and now the democratic parliament. 'The Dream of the **Rood**' is a poem inscribed in runes on the Ruthwell Cross in Dumfries and Galloway dating back to *c.* 700.

rooked   cleaned out, broke, penniless.

roup   auction. If you are **brought to the roup**, you are bankrupt and your goods and belongings are being auctioned.

rovies   slippers: '**Jings!** Whit a **tumshie**. Ah've come oot fur ma **messages** still in ma **rovies!**' Also known as 'baffies'.

rowan   the mountain ash (*Sorbus aucupariaa*). A rowan tree planted in a garden is said to bring luck to the house.

rowie or **buttery**   a morning roll popular in Aberdeen and the north-east. It doesn't contain butter but – in true Scots healthy-eating tradition – is 49 per cent lard. Any topping must always be added to the flat side.

rumgumption   common sense.
> *(For manners ne'er could awe them*
> *Frae their presumption)*
> *They need not try thy jokes to fathom,*
> *They want **rumgumption**.*
James Beattie, 'To Mr Alexander Ross', *c.* 1775

rumbledethumps   a delicious mixture of mashed **tatties, ingins** and cabbage.

runkle   crinkle, crease or scrunch up.

runrig   field system for ensuring **crofters** got a fair chance of the best (and worst) agricultural land over time, the land being divided into strips or **rigs** allocated by lot.

rushyroo   shrew (*Soricidae*).

S

Selkirk bannock

saft   out-dated word for a gentle person lacking mental vigour: 'He's **saft** in the **heid**.' A Scotsman showing actual emotion might be called 'a **big saftie**'.

saining   to purify with fire or water, especially at the start of a new venture or journey, such as the move to the summer **shielings** or a new fishing season. See also **clavie**.

sair heidie   a sponge cake from Aberdeenshire sold in a paper wrapper; looks like a bandaged head.

saltire   the St Andrew's Cross, a white diagonal cross on a field of blue, the national flag of Scotland. St Andrew asked to be crucified diagonally, feeling not worthy to be martyred on an upright cross as Christ had been.

Samhain [*sow-ain* or *sa-wain*]   the old fire festival that marked the end of summer and beginning of winter on 31 October; now integrated into Hallowe'en. See also **Beltane**.

sang   song. At the dissolution of the Scots parliament in 1707 the Earl of Seafield commented, 'There's an end to ane auld **sang**.' A 'sang schule' is a music school. In medieval cathedrals a **precentor** was responsible for the education and training of boys for the choir in the sang schule.

sarking   the wooden boards or planks covering the rafters and underneath the slates on a roof.

sassenach [*sass-en-ach*] (Gaelic)   originally meaning 'Lowlander' or 'Saxon', now used, if at all, by Scots to describe an Englander. Used in *Outlander* as a nickname for the time-travelling English nurse.

scaffie   1. municipal dump, rubbish heap; 2. bin lorry, refuse truck; 3. street sweeper.

scart   1. scrape or claw; 2. shag (*Phalacrocorax aristotelis*).

'Albino Example of Shag or **Scart** – I am presenting to the Royal Scottish Museum a white **Scart** shot by me on the west coast of Isle of Barra on the 16th September 1924.'
John Beaton, Barra, in *The Scottish Naturalist*, 1924

scheme   a twentieth-century public housing development, usually on the edge of a city, where residents of densely packed and unhygienic inner-city slum dwellings were rehoused by municipal councils. However, by the end of the century many such estates were being blighted by wider post-industrial social problems. Hotbeds of vibrant Scots words and language. A 'schemie' is a derogatory name for someone from a **scheme**, usually implying lack of education, unemployment and/or alcohol or drug addiction.

sclaff   a glancing blow. In **fitba** or **golf** if you **sclaff** the ball, you mishit it.

scone [*sk-awn*, not *sk-oon*]   a tasty afternoon treat made from flour, eggs, sugar, milk and baking powder, baked in an oven. Cheese can be substituted for sugar for a savoury **scone**. See **Stone of Scone**.

Scotch   1. of Scotland. Scot or Scots have now generally replaced **Scotch** in common usage as descriptions of people from Scotland, although it is used to describe foodstuffs, for example, **Scotch broth**, a barley-based soup, or **Scotch pie**; 2. whisky distilled in Scotland – but not called that in Scotland. See also **dram** and **usquebaugh**. To summarise: A Scot, perhaps descended from the Scots, speaks Scots, whose nationality is Scottish, would sup Scotch broth but wouldn't order a 'Scotch' at the bar.

Scotch pie   a small, round, hand-held pie for one made of minced mutton and offal encased in hot water pastry. See also **peh**.

Scots Greys   cavalry regiment mounted on white or grey horses. See also **Louseland**.

Scotticism   a word or phrase comprising standard English words but with a uniquely Scottish usage: 'Did you get the **messages**?', '**Riding the marches**'.

Scottishness   Scottish characteristic, best summed up in this classic line:
> 'Basically, we live a short, disappointing life; and then we die.
> We fill up oor lives wi shite, things like careers and relationships
> tae delude oorsels that it isnae aw totally pointless.'
>
> Irvine Welsh, *Trainspotting*, 1994

scramble   the frenetic collection of small coins thrown to waiting children by a departing groom following a wedding service. On one occasion Granpaw in **The Broons** wears kneepads to a wedding to better participate in the **scramble** afterwards, the rest of the family being suitably **black-affrontit**.

scratcher, see **Louseland**.

scrieve   to write.
> '**Scrievin** in Scots ebbs an flows lik the tide. We're ackwally in a
> verra fertile time the nou fir writin in wir ain leid.'
>
> Rab Wilson, *The National* newspaper, 12 April 2018

scud   naked: 'Wrinkly? They went loony **dookin**' in the scud.'

sculduddery   lewd or obscene behaviour or words. The *Dictionary of the Scots Language* notes that it is the root of the word 'skulduggery': 'The word appeared in U.S. about the end of the nineteenth century in the form skulduggery with the meaning of misappropriation of funds, fraud.'

scunner   confound, perplex, bemuse, disgust.
> '[The Minister] next asked the young woman, or the bride,
> if she was willing to take the young man to be her lawful

husband? when she answered "No, sir!" "What . . . are your reasons?" asked the worthy divine. "O," replied she, hanging down her head, "I have just ta'en a **scunner** [disgust] at him."

The Scotch Haggis: a miscellaneous compilation, illustrative of Scottish wit, 1875

See you, Jimmy　a supposedly common, unnecessarily aggressive phrase used by Scots; popular with late-twentieth-century English comedians. A 'See you, Jimmy hat' is a tartan tammy (see **Tam o'Shanter**) with ginger-hair wig attached, a hilariously witty garb adored by tourists, especially if accompanied by a **tartan** towel designed to look like the **kilt**. Oh, how we Scots laugh (as we pocket the cash).

selkie　in folklore, a seal that undergoes metamorphosis into a human when on land and vice versa.

*I am a man upon the land, I am a **silkie** in the sea,*
But when I'm in my own coutrie
*My dwelling is in Sule **skerrie**.'*

'The Great Seal of Sule Skerrie', traditional

Selkirk bannock　a heavily fruited round loaf from the Borders.

semmit　vest. Compare the attractiveness of TV character Rab C. Nesbitt's string **semmit** with the allure of Nannie's **cutty** sark chemise in 'Tam o' Shanter'.

'In cases of tuberculosis, the patient's **semmit** (vest) was boiled with a conger eel and was then taken straight from the pot and worn at all times, day and night.'

Review of Scottish Culture, 2008

sgian-dhu/skean-dhu (Gaelic)　black knife or dagger, now worn tucked into the top of a sock as part of a **kilt**'s accessories.

shairn/sharn　cow manure.

'Ane cow . . . milked nothing but water, quhilk stinked and
tasted of **sharn** a long tyme.'
Shetland Witch Trials, 1644

shan   weak, damaged, poor quality, worn.

shanky/shunkey   toilet. Shanks of Barhead were famous makers of
sanitary ware.
'Mick's in the **shunkey**, where he spends half his life, tossing
himself off.'
Robin Jenkins, *Just Duffy*, 1988

sharger (Gaelic, *sairg*)   person or creature who is weak or puny, perhaps through starvation or illness.

shauchle   shuffle, walk without lifting one's feet.

shaw   wood, copse. My grandfather would refer to 'the queer folk o'
the Shaws', the term originating from the settlement of exiled French
Protestant weavers in the Pollokshaws in the early eighteenth century.
Then it was a rural, wooded area outside Glasgow.

shed   parting, as in hair. Originally an agricultural term for dividing
calves from cows and lambs from ewes.

sheep's heid   considered a delicacy above French cooking by Sir Walter
Scott:
'I wish for a sheep's head and whisky toddy against all the
French cookery and champagne in the world.'
Sir Walter Scott, *The Journal of Sir Walter Scott*, 1890

And there'll be partens and buckles, [crabs and whelks]
And whytens and speldins enew, [herring]

*And singit **sheep-heads** and a **haggis**,*
*And **scaldips** to sup till ye spew.* [mutton and barley broth]
Robert Semple of Beltrees, 'The Wedding of Maggie and Jock', *c.* 1650

sheltie   Shetland pony, a diminutive breed of working horse suited for island life. Its long-maned attractiveness as a cute learner horse for girls keen on riding and lower maintenance cost for their parents has meant that as a breed it has found a new lease of life where other Scottish working horses, such as the Lewis pony (like Scots agricultural and crofting words), have gone extinct.

shenachie [*shen-ach-ee*] (Gaelic, *seanachaidh*)   formerly a keeper of a **clan**'s, family's or community's history, genealogy and traditions, usually orally and from memory. May now refer to someone with a wide knowledge and understanding of Gaelic culture.

Sheriff Court   the court that deals with most civil and less serious criminal cases, three years in prison being the maximum sentence it can hand down. A sheriff is a judge or magistrate in the court; a sheriff principal is the leading sheriff in an area; and a sheriff officer is a bailiff who acts on behalf of a sheriff delivering summonses to court and collecting debts and fines.

sherrackin'   bawling out, a serious verbal reprimand.
'That strange and wild appeal to crowd justice and crowd sympathy which Glasgow describes as a **"sherrieking"**.'
Alexander McArthur and Herbert Kingsley Long, *No Mean City*, 1935

sheugh   drain, ditch, gutter; hence, the cleft of the buttocks is known as the **sheugh** of your arse.

shieling   once the annual summertime home on hill or moor for crofters and smallholders, each with a designated site where cattle would be grazed on upland rough pasture and plants, herbs, fruits, mosses and lichens collected for foods, medicines and dyes.

shilling 70/shilling 80/shilling . . .   old amount of tax on beer, still used as indicative of strength or alcohol content.

shilpit   puny: 'Yon's a **shilpit wee nyaff**.'

shiner   black eye.

shinty   one of many ancient stick-and-ball games. Its roots lie in hurling and the sixth-, seventh- and eighth-century spread of Christianity into Scotland from Ireland. See also **caman**.

shith/sith [*shee*] (Gaelic)   the fairy folk; occurs in placenames such as Glen **Shee** and Schiehallion – the hill of the **Caledonian** fairies.

shoogle   give a shake; **shoogly** is wobbly, unsteady. A **fitba** manager with a string of poor recent results could be described as 'Hae'in' her job on a **shoogly** peg.'

shoot the craw   to hasten away or flee the scene (sometimes without having paid for goods or services). To have 'shot amang the craws' means to have mixed in bad company and so be punished along with them.

shortbread/shortie   biscuit traditionally given as a **first foot** at **Hogmanay** and **Ne'er Day**. Tins of **shortbread** are synonymous with unrealistically romanticised views and images of Scotland.

shot   go, turn: 'It's my **shot** on the **sheltie**!'

shows   fairground attractions: 'Kirkcaldy Links Market has a mile of **shows** alang the esplanade each year.'

shunkey, see **shanky**.

shy   throw, especially a throw-in at **fitba**.

siccar sure, certain. After Robert the Bruce had stabbed John Comyn of Badenoch (known as the Red) in a Dumfries church in 1306, his cousin Kirkpatrick said, 'I'll mak **siccar**,' and went back and stabbed him again.

silk napkin rainbow of which only a portion can be seen. See also **watergaw**.

silver darlings herring.
> 'They forgot all about the ship; they forgot everything, except
> the herrings, the lithe silver fish, the swift flashing ones,
> hundreds and thousands of them, the **silver darlings**.'
> Neil M. Gunn, *The Silver Darlings*, 1941

simmer dim Shetland term for long summer evenings where due to the northern latitude it never really gets dark at night.

single end a single-roomed apartment, usually in a **tenement**, without an inside toilet.

sith, see **shith**.

sitooterie dining premises with al fresco facilities.

skail spill, leave. Dancers will **skail** out of the hall at the end of a **ceilidh**.

skean-dhu, see **sgian-dhu**.

skeich [*skeech*] 1. an excitable child or beast full of nervous energy; 2. a pensioner with more-than-natural amounts of energy.

skelf splinter of wood lodged under the skin.

skellie off-centre: 'She turned hersel' **skellie** wi' ridin' on every **show** at the Links Market.'

skelp   slap: 'He's got a face like a well-**skelped** bum.'

skerries/skerry   rocky outcrop in the sea. See also **selkie**.

skiddle   mess about, usually splashing about with or in water.

skinnymalink   tall, thin person.
> *Skinymalinky lang legs,*
> *Umber-ella feet,*
> *Went to the pictures*
> *And fell right through the seat!*
> Children's skipping song, traditional

skirl   the rousing sound of the **bagpipes**: 'The **skirl** o' the pipes.'

skirlie   fried onions in oatmeal. The sound it makes in the pan resembles the **skirl** o' the pipes.

skite   slip, slide: 'Och, I **skited** on the **sheugh** o' my arse!'

skitter   run fast but chaotically; thus, suffering from diarrhoea is known as having the **skitters**.

skliff   1. scuff the soles of your shoes on the ground to make a noise; 2. the noise made by **skliffing**.

skoosh   fizzy carbonated soft drink. See also **juice**.

skulduggery, see **sculduddery**.

slabber   drool, be of slovenly appearance and habits. See also **slaister**.

slainte/slainte mhath [*slange/slan-ja-vah*] (Gaelic, 'good health')   a toast, cheers!

slaister   person making a mess.
> 'Mistakes were made on both sides, in the confusion and
> **slaister** of mud.'
> Nigel Tranter, *The Story of Scotland*, 1987

slattyvarrie (Gaelic, *slatmhara*)   edible seaweed.

sleekit   sly, smooth, ingratiating (definitions that sit at odds with its
most famous usage, that of smooth/sleek).
> *Wee, **sleekit**, couran, tim'rous beastie,*
> *O, what a panic's in thy breastie!*
> Robert Burns, 'To a Mouse', 1785

sleuch   to slurp noisily while drinking from a spoon or a straw (or even
a saucer).

slider   scoop of ice cream sandwiched between two wafers.

slip-ma-laaber   work-shy Shetlander.

slitter   1. to eat or drink messily; 2. a messy eater or drinker: 'You're a
slabbering, slitter of a **slaister**.'

slogan   a Highland, **clan** or family war cry, hence the modern universal
meaning as a strapline or motto to identify a brand. See also **caberfeidh**.
> 'The name of Hume have for their **slughorn** (or **slogan** as our
> southern shires terme it) "a Hume", "a Hume".'
> Sir George Mackenzie of Rosehaugh, *The science of herauldry treated
> as part of the civil law and law of nations, etc.*, 1680

slunge   rinse under a tap (rather than wash): 'Ye **slittering slaister!** Yiv
slabbered doon yir **semmit** eating yon **slider** in the **sitooterie**. Gie it a
slunge.'

smashing (Gaelic, *'s math sin*, 'that is good')   super, great.

smeddum (Old English, *smedema*, the best essence at the heart of a substance, especially ground flour) grit, endurance allied to knowledge; determination with a sense of right. Lewis Grassic Gibbon entitled a short story 'Smeddum', and the word also appears in his novel *Cloud Howe*.

'. . . and mabe there were better folk far in Segget, but few enough with **smeddum** like his.'

Lewis Grassic Gibbon, *Cloud Howe*, 1933

smiddy blacksmiths, forge. See **Gretna Green**.

smirr a fine misty rain.

'The rain that was a **smirr** or drizzle on the north side of Glencoe grew to a steady shower in the valley itself.'

Neil Munro, *John Splendid*, 1898

smit/smote 1. to infect; 2. to hit.

'Ever trew and obedient bayth to God and the Prince, without any **smote**.'

John Knox, *c.* 1556

smoor to draw in the ashes of a fire to keep it lit but burning low, especially overnight. It would traditionally be the matriarch of the house's job to **smoor** the fire at night, perhaps making the sign of the cross in the ashes and saying a prayer.

*I will **smoor** the hearth*
*As Mary would **smoor**;*
The encompassnient of Bride and of Mary,
On the fire and on the floor.
And on the household all.

Alexander Carmichael, 'Smooring Blessing', 1992

smowt youngster, technically a young trout or salmon but also affectionately applied to a child.

sna' aff a dyke   literally, 'snow off a wall', something that is momentary. 'Although the money came in . . . it would go like the **snow off a dyke**.'
John Galt, *Annals of the Parish*, 1821

snash   cheek, answering back: 'Dinnae **snash** yir mither!'

sneck   1. the lock on a door or gate; 2. the act of putting on the catch of a lock so the door is closed but can be opened without a key; see also **snib**.

snib   1. a lock on a door or window; 2. the act of locking or bolting, as opposed to **sneck**.

snochters/snotters   nasal mucus. A **snochter-dichter** is a handkerchief. See also **Airdrie hankie**.

sodie-heid   literally, 'head full of soda bubbles', airhead.

sonsie/sonsy (Gaelic, *sonas*, 'good fortune')   attractive, thriving; applied to a woman or a **haggis**.
'Nae gentleman wad plunder a leddy and a right **sonsy** damsel too.'
Tobias Smollett, *The Reprisal*, 1757

sook/souk   1. a sycophant, teacher's pet; 2. to ingratiate; 3. suck or soak up (liquid).

soom   1. swim; 2. flood: 'The **stairheid** was **soomin'** in water after the leak.'

soop   sweep, specifically in the sport of **curling** to smooth the ice before the moving stone to make it travel faster.

soor douk   literally, 'sour faced'; misery guts.

soor ploom   literally, 'sour plum'; boiled sweet with tart fruity taste.

sooth-moother   Shetland term for incomer from the south.

sort   mend, fix, repair.
> 'See it. Say it. **Sorted**.'
> Scotrail travel safety **slogan**

souch/sough   the sound of wind, the rustling of leaves or swish of birds' wings.
> *As thay* [swans] *returne thar weyngis **souchand** jolely.*
> Gavin Douglas, *The Aeneid*, 1513

souk paps   sea anemones (*Actiniaria*).

soutar/souter   cobbler, shoemaker. '**Souter** Johnny' is **Tam o'Shanter**'s 'ancient, trusty, **drouthy** crony' in Burns' poem.

spaewife (Norse, *spa*, 'foretell')   fortune teller, seer.

speir   ask.
> 'Policeman: Fat's yir name?
>   Janet: Fat the deil needs yi **speir** a silly question o' that kin?
> Ye ken my name weel enuch.'
> J. Derrick McClure, *Doric: The Dialect of North-East Scotland*, 2002

speug   sparrow (*Passer domesticus*).

spinnle trams   thin, spindle-like legs.

sporran   man's leather pouch strung on a belt, usually made of both leather and chain, worn in front of the **kilt**. It will usually have a flapped lid and be decorated with leather tassels, with fur or hide often used on the front portion. But while size and decoration vary, anything too large or over-elaborate might be seen as **tartanry**.

sprag   boast, sprawl or swagger: 'He's a total **sprag**, manspreading on the train.'

spuilzie [*spool-yee*], (Old French, *espoillier*, 'to spoil')   plunder, steal.

spurtle   wooden kitchen implement for stirring porridge.

square go   a fight with no weapons; squaring up one to one.

square sausage, see **Lorne sausage**.

stair   Scots use the singular for a flight of stairs. In a **tenement** you will take a turn to clean the **stair**. A landing on or at the top of the **stair** is a **stairheid**. As intermediate, communal ground, it is a place where conversations and interactions of all types take place.

stammygaster   a north-eastern word for astonishment or surprise, usually unpleasant.

stank   metal drain cover. In Glasgow a very thin person is advisedly called a **stank dodger**.

stank hen   moorhen (*Gallinula chloropus*).

stappit/stappit fu   full to the brim, no more room, stuffed. See also **stowed oot**.

stave   sprain, twist or jar: 'A've **staved** ma fing-er.'

steamie   in nineteenth- and twentieth-century cities, a communal laundry or wash house; a female space where help, advice, news and gossip could be exchanged. Even today if you are the subject of scandal you can be referred to as 'the talk of the **steamie**!'

steel bonnets, see **reivers**.

stewartry   land under the stewardship of a person appointed by the monarch, for example, the **Stewartry** of Kirkcudbright. The Stewart kings and queens were descended from Walter, made High Steward of Scotland in 1150. Stewart is a fine example of the Scots pronunciation of the glottal stop.

stey   steep: 'Set a stout heart against a **stey brae**.'

stinking Billy   Jacobite name for the flower sweet William. William 'The Butcher', Duke of Cumberland, led the victorious government forces at the Battle of Culloden in 1746 and the subsequent bloody suppression of dissent in the Highlands.

stoat/stot   jump about, bounce, sometimes travel hither. If you are **stoatin'**, you are drunkenly bouncing along.

stoatir   Glaswegian appreciation of beauty, usually feminine beauty: 'Yon Aphrodite McGlumpher's a **wee stoatir!**'

stob   1. (Gaelic [*stop*]) point, usually as part of a hill name: **Stob** Binnein, **Stob** Coire nan Lochan; 2. [*stob*] a nail, spike or fence post.

Stone of Scone [*skoon*] or **Stone of Destiny**   ancient rock on which the Scottish monarch was crowned at Scone near Perth. It was removed by the invading English King Edward I in 1296 and incorporated into the English, later British, Coronation Throne in Westminster Abbey, London, thus becoming a symbol of oppression or unity depending on your viewpoint. Famously repatriated by a group of Scottish students on Christmas Day 1950. Eventually it was returned – but was it the real stone that went back? Doubts still remain. Public pressure with the rise of Scottish nationalism saw the Stone permanently returned in 1996 and it now sits in Edinburgh Castle.

> *The Dean o' Westminster was a powerful man*
> *He held a' the strings o' the State in his hand*

> *But wi' a' his great business it flustered him nane*
> *When some rogues ran away wi' his wee magic stane.*
> Johnny McEvoy, 'The Wee Magic Stane', 1951

stookie　plaster cast protecting a broken limb, from *stucco*, plaster of Paris.

stool of repentence　a seat in a **kirk** where those found guilty of sinning – usually illicit fornication – would be made to sit apart from the rest of the congregation and then lectured on their lack of morals by the minister at the end of a Sunday service. Fear and shame of it led many women to conceal their pregnancies, with tragic results.

stooshie　to-do, commotion or uproar: 'Oh there was a right **stooshie** last night. Steamin an' **sooked** the **stairheid**! She wis the talk o' the **steamie**, the morn.'

stourie　1. dusty; 2. in a fog or mist, perhaps of forgetfulness or disorientation; 3. confrontation or commotion. Scottish coal miners would suffer from **stourie lungs**.

stovies　a dish with potatoes cooked on a stove on top of onions, with a meat gravy in one pot or dish, thus steaming the potatoes with the flavours from beneath them.

stowed oot　very busy; see also **stappit fu**.

stramash　conflict, chaotic fight or scramble. Though used by poets, it will always be associated with 1970s **fitba** commentators such as Arthur Montford or David Francey describing 'a **stramash** in the penalty box'.

strath (Gaelic, *srath*)　river valley, as in placenames such as Strathearn and Strathmore. It can also denote a wider area. Strathclyde has been used as the name for the ancient kingdom stretching from north-west England to Loch Lomond and the former local-government area covering much of west central Scotland.

strathspey   both a type of slow **reel** dance and the music in four-four time that accompanies it; named after the river valley where it originated.

stravaig   go awandering, carefree, or shirking responsibility.

sugarallie (from 'sugar-alicreesh', licorice)   an old-fashioned soft drink made by dissolving sugar and licorice in water; used to describe any overly sweet drink.

> '**Bairns** gaily shook their bottles of **sugarelly** water into a froth.'
> J. M. Barrie, *A Window in Thrums*, 1889

swally   literally, 'swallow'; hence, to drink alcohol. See also **bevvy**.

swatch [*swA-tch*]   look at: 'Gie's a **swatch** at volume 9 of yon *A Dictionary of the Older Scottish Tongue* when yiv feenished.'

syne   since. 'For **Auld Lang Syne**' literally translates to 'old long since', meaning 'for old times' sake'.

T

tattie bogle

tablet   a sweet made from sugar, butter, milk and condensed milk melted in a pan, poured into a baking tray to cool, then cut into squares. Very Scottish – extreme over-sweetness (sinful) combined with hints of fundamentalist instruction of the Ten Commandments (tablets of Moses).

tackety   studded with tacks or seggs, especially on the soles of boots. Schoolchildren would delight in **sclaffing** them along the street to create sparks.

tak tent   take heed; a warning given to someone with notions of going against some greater power or authority – human, natural or supernatural.

Tally   Italian. With many late-nineteenth-century Italian immigrants to Scotland opening cafes selling ice-cream, the raspberry sauce poured on cones was popularly known as **Tally's blood**.

Tam o'Shanter   1. a sublime poetic visualisation of Everyman created by the incomparable genius of Robert Burns; 2. the eponymous hero of the poem; 3. a type of Scotch bonnet like a beret with a pom-pom on top, popularly said to have been worn by him, sometimes called a toorie, a tammy or, if patterned, a tartan tammy; see **tartanry** and '**See you, Jimmy**'.

tammy-nid-nod   tadpole.

tangle   seaweed, usually *Laminaria digitata*, found on Scotland's shores and traditionally used to fertilise poor coastal land for small-scale domestic agriculture; later harvested industrially as a source of potash and iodine.

tappit-hen   either the notched lid or the whole of a (usually pewter) traditional beer tankard. From the crest on top of a hen or cockerel's head.

tapsalteerie   topsy-turvy, upside-down.

tarry-fingert [*fing-ert* – a beautiful word to pronounce]   a thief.

tartan   1. (noun) a woollen checked cloth woven of different coloured threads dyed using local natural colours, thought to have originated in the Highlands. Its wearing was banned following the eighteenth-century **Jacobite** uprisings. A spurious and romantic history was then imposed on it. Whatever its past, it is forever associated with Scotland; 2. (adjective) used to describe a Scottish variant, e.g. **tartan army** or **tartan Tories** (a label given by its leftist opponents to the Scottish National Party, implying it is just a Scottish version of the right-wing British Conservative Party). See also **tinker's tartan**.

tartan army   collective name for supporters of the Scottish national **fitba** (we don't call it soccer) team who actually attend matches, home and away. Use is often self-congratulatory of their exemplary behaviour, in comparison with the hooliganism of English fans (if you find drunken indecent exposure by kilt-wearers within your idea of acceptable behaviour in the twenty-first century). Given to over-optimism and **tartanry**.

Tartan Day   6 April celebration of Scottish roots by Americans and ex-pat Scots.

tartanry   term for over-elaborate interpretation of authentic Scottish culture or customs, especially dress – what my granny would call 'bumbee tartan'. The identification of what *is* 'authentic' is somewhat open to interpretation.

tassie (Old French, *tasse*, 'cup')   cup or goblet, usually a sporting trophy, for example the 'Craw's Nest Tassie' played for annually at Carnoustie Golf Course.

tatterdemalion   ill-clad person, dressed in rags. The **Jacobite** army of 1745 was described by the double agent James Gilchrist as 'a pack of

tatterdemalions . . . marching without breeches, stockings, or shoes'. See also **flapdawdron, tattie bogle**.

tattie   potato. Its introduction was so successful in the smallhold-ing crofting communities of northern and western Scotland that when affected by blight in the 1840s and 1850s the devastation saw depopula-tion and emigration of a third of the community. See also **clapshot** and **mince 'n' tatties**.

tattie scone   potato scone; thinner, flatter and quartered compared to a traditional **scone**, usually an accompaniment to a fry-up or Scottish breakfast, along with bacon, sausage, egg, **haggis**, black pudding, etc.

tattie bogle   scarecrow; literally, 'potato ghost'. Also used to describe a person of dishevelled and unkempt appearance. See also **flapdawdron, tatterdemalion**.

tattie holidays   pre-mechanisation, traditionally, two October weeks off school for children in Scotland's agricultural communities in order to harvest the potato crop – anything but a holiday. The act of pulling up the potatoes is known as 'tattie howkin".

tawse   the 'belt'; a thick, two-pronged leather strap, the favoured form of corporal punishment in Scottish schools until it was banned in 1987. Its effectiveness and use depended on the quality of the teacher rather than pupil.

tea-jenny   a prolific drinker of tea.

team   a gang; for example, Govan Young **Team**. Also 'fleet', such as Lorne Auld Fleet.

tee-name   in areas where generations of children were given traditional family names, a **tee-name** was used to distinguish individuals, especially in the north-east and in Gàidhealtachd, where the TV presenter Donnie

B. McLeod did not have a middle name beginning with B but was one of many with the same name: Donnie A. McLeod, Donnie C. McLeod, etc. This is not so much an issue in the twenty-first century if you are called Adora-Belle or Lucifer – though one Scottish school reputedly has two pupils called Unique.

telling   given sage advice or a scolding. When someone argues back after being given this feedback, they might be told to 'take a **telling**'.

telt   having received a **telling**, see above. It might also suggest a physical as well as a verbal correction has been issued.

tenement   originally, a plot of land; contemporary definition includes the apartment block built on it. Tenements in nineteenth- and twentieth-century cities could range from notorious high-density slums to **douce** middle-class residences. When he first came to Glasgow in the nineteenth century, a man from the remote island of St Kilda could not believe that horses wore shoes or that people lived inside cliffs.

teri/teerie   native of the **Borders** town of Hawick; origin unknown but it is featured in a tune played annually at the **common riding**.

term day, see **quarter day**.

terr   fun times: 'It's rerr **terr** at Err at ra **Ferr**' ['One has uniquely fun times in the seaside resort of Ayr in July during the Glasgow **trades** fortnight holidays'].

teuchit   lapwing (*Vanellus cristatus*); also known as a peewit. In the north-east the **teuchit** or **gowk** storm is a spell of wintery weather in early spring.

teuchter   condescending, casually insulting name used by Lowlanders to mockingly describe someone from the Highlands; thankfully, if slowly, falling out of use. See also **heuchter-teuchter**.

thirl (Old Scots)   to pierce with a weapon.
   *. . . my sheild **thirlit** with stalwart spiers.*
   The Buik of the Most Noble and Valiant Conqueror Alexander the Grit,
   early fifteenth century

thistle   the national plant. Legend has it the Scottish nation was secured after a Viking warrior stood on a prickly thistle and yelped, giving away the Norwegian position at the Battle of Largs in 1263. Nothing to do with our flourishing on poor soil, prickly natures, brief periods of flowering and dispersal of our seed far and wide. See also **jag**.

thole   endure. Scots excel at enduring.

thon   that; often used to avoid naming a person or thing out of disgust, disrespect or fear: '**Thon!**'

thrang   crowded, densely packed.
   The daft and gleesom bands
   That fill Edina's streets,
   *Sae **thrang** this day.*
   Not during the present-day Edinburgh Festival but in Robert
   Fergusson's poem, 'Leith Races', 1773

thrapple   throat or gullet.
   The great muckle village of Balmaquhapple?
   *'Tis **steep'd** in iniquity up to the **thrapple**.*
   James Hogg, 'The Village of Balmaquhapple', 1831

thrawn   twisted, surly, obstinate. '**Thrawn** Janet' in Robert Louis Stevenson's 1881 short story is in league with the devil.

thrums   leftovers; derives from any threads remaining on the loom after the weaving has been removed.

thunner-plump   heavy downpour or rain during a thunderstorm; liable to leave one **drookit**.

tinker's tartan   blotching of the skin caused by Scotland's weather – cold, wind and rain.

tirve   steal, remove. 'To **tirve** the **kirk** to theek the quire' is 'to rob Peter to pay Paul'.

tod   fox (*Vulpes vulpes*).

toom   empty. **Toom Tabbard** is the nickname given to John Balliol, installed as king of Scotland by Edward I of England in 1292. Balliol was 'empty' in two senses: firstly as a vassal to the enemy he was a king of no substance; then, when he rebelled, Edward stripped him of the monarchy, and Balliol's surcoat, which had previously borne the royal arms of Scotland, was left without a design.

torn-faced   having an unhappy or disgruntled look: 'She wis aye a **torn-faced besom**.'

tourist eagle   buzzard (*Buteo buteo*), common raptor frequently mistaken for the very rare golden eagle by the wishful-thinking visitor.

tousie   tangled, unkempt.
> *His breast was white, his **touzie** back*
> *Weel clad wi' coat o' glossy black . . .*
> Robert Burns, 'The Twa Dogs', 1786

tow   corded material, for example, rope, string, hawser.

trades   collective name for the organised craft workers in a burgh who would regulate terms and conditions for work from apprenticeships to toll duties. Still used to describe a municipality's annual summer holiday period; see **terr**.

trauchle   a task that is troublesome, weary or dull to do: 'Rounding up the **haggis** is a real **trauchle**.'

trews   combo of **kilt** and **breeks**, trousers made of **tartan** material. Neither Highland nor Lowland, this **tartanry** hybrid was a favoured dress of 1970s fascist punks and still of officers in the Scottish army.

tron   the public weighing scales of a medieval Scottish burgh; hence a centre of trade, such as the **Trongate** in Glasgow.

trow   troll or mischief-making imp, especially in the Northern Isles.

tube   an idiot or someone doing something stupid. See also **tumshie**.

tulchan (Gaelic, *tulachan*)   a calf-skin filled with straw to encourage a cow to keep producing milk.

tumble   shake up: 'Yid better tak a **tumble** to yirsel' if yi want tae pass yir Highers.'

tummle yir wilkies   to fall head over heels; literally meaning to twist like a wild cat.

tumshie   turnip. Also known as 'neep'. Often used to describe a foolish person or in a chastisement for their foolish actions or behaviours: 'Ya **tumshie**!'

tup   ram. To be **tup-heidit** is to be stubborn and obstinate.
   'Instead it was Archie who stood inside the door, lips tight and naked head glaring and said, "Ye senseless bluidy **tup-heidit** madman!" with venom.'
   Dorothy Dunnett, *Checkmate*, 1975

tweed   heavy cloth woven using homespun wool and coloured using naturally obtained dyes. Harris Tweed with the orb and cross trademark must be manufactured on the Western Isles.

'Since the great Depression had begun to creep in on us –
its grimy tentacles reaching out across the Minch from the
cities and searching us out even in our remote corner – the
Harris **Tweed** trade had collapsed, and yards upon yards of
beautiful **tweed** that had been spun with toil and woven
with high hope were now stacked unsold in every corner of
the house, as symbolic of the times as the rusting hulks on
Clydeside.'

Finlay J. MacDonald, *Crowdie and Cream*, 1982

two New Years   the opportunity to celebrate according to both the Gregorian and Julian calendars; see **Auld Yule**.

'Cairndow . . . where they keep the **two New Years**.'

Neil Munro, *Para Handy*, 1906

Up-Helly-Aa

uisge beatha, see **usquebaugh**.

Unco   1. unusual, unnatural, strange; 2. extremely; '**unco** guid' in Burns' poem of that name refers to the sanctimonious and self-righteous.

Union, the   the Union of the Parliaments of Scotland and England in 1707.

> 'He castigated Belhaven for his impassioned defence of Scottish
> independence in the Scottish Parliament in November 1706;
> only by **union** with England, [the writer and spy Daniel] Defoe
> urged, would the Sots find the happiness and prosperity that
> existed in Holland.'
> Christopher A. Whatley, *Scots and the Union*, 2014

Up-Helly-Aa   Shetland festival held on the last Tuesday in January celebrating the island's Norse heritage; **guisers** in Viking costume elect a 'jarl' to lead the 'jarl squad' with flaming torches thrown into a reconstructed longship after a night-time parade through Lerwick, the capital. A nineteenth-century construct – like its 'men-only' rule.

uplift   collect; for example, put the bins out for **uplift**.

uppie-killie-donkey   to ride a see-saw on Orkney.

upsitten (Old Scots)   an animal sitting or resting on its haunches. For the Protestant **Covenanters** it could be used to describe someone lacking their fundamentalist zealotry.

> 'Those who have fallen in contentedly with this backsliding and
> **upsitten** church . . . These backslidden, **upsitten**, lukewarm
> Ministers, Elders and Professors . . .'
> Patrick Walker, *The Life of Peden*, 1728

urlar (Gaelic, 'floor')   in **bagpipe** music this is the basis on which the **pibroch** is constructed.

urnae am/are not: 'I say, my **trews** are absolutely splendid!' '**Urnae**.'

usquebaugh/uisge beatha (Gaelic, 'the water of life') whisky. Alcoholic drink made from distilling water with: 1. malted barley in a pot still for **malt** whisky; 2. other unmalted grain such as maize in a patent still for grain whisky; 3. a combination of the two for blended whisky. Peat is usually a key ingredient either in the water source or burned as a fuel in the malting process. Sometimes called 'cratur', meaning creature, endowing whisky with the properties of an animate being and thus emphasising its unique qualities. Also known as a **dram**, fuskie, a measure and **Scotch**, but never whiskey.

> 'Ach, he's feeling the shortage of whisky. We're all feeling it, Sergeant. Never mind. Good things will come again, and we'll have whisky galore. **Uisge beatha** gu leoirl.'
> Compton Mackenzie, *Whisky Galore*, 1947

V

velvet-coated gentleman

vatted malt   a mix of malt whiskies.

vaunty   proud. See also **vogie**.
And Mysie wha's clavering Aunty
*Wad match her wi' Laurie the **laird**,*
*And learns the young fuel to be **vaunty**,*
But neither to spin nor to card.
Joanna Baillie, 'Fy let us a' to the Wedding', 1827

velvet-coated gentleman   mole (*Talpa europaea*); also known as a 'moudiewart'. **Jacobites** would raise a glass to the **velvet-coated gentleman** as their nemesis King William II – also associated with the **Glencoe** massacre – died after his horse stumbled in a mole-hole. See also **the king over the water**.

vennel (French, *venelle*)   a lane or outdoor close between buildings. The **Vennel** in Edinburgh runs up from the Grassmarket beside the Flodden Wall, built after the disastrous defeat of King James IV by the English in 1513.

visek (Norwegian, *vise*)   song sung to a circular dance.
'A dozen or so form themselves into a circle, and taking each other by the hand, perform a sort of circular dance, one of the company all the while singing a Norn **Visick**.'
George Low, *A Tour through the Islands of Orkney and Shetland*, 1774

visiting cough   a cold or flu suffered by inhabitants of the remote island of St Kilda brought on by being exposed to and infected by germs carried by visitors, against which they had no resistance.

vogie   proud, elated. See also **vaunty**.
We took a spring, and danc'd a fling,
*And wow but we were **vogie**!*

> *We didna fear, though we lay near*
> *The Campbells, in Stra'bogie.*
> James Hogg, *The Jacobite Relics of Scotland*, 1819–21

vratch   wretch (north-east): 'Supports Aiberdeen, he's aye been a puir
vratch.'

webster

wabbit   feeling under the weather with no precise symptoms. See also **wersh**.

wabster, see **webster**.

wallie/wally   originally, pretty or ornamental; now, glazed china, for example, the tiles in a **tenement** close or ornamental porcelain **wally dugs** on the ends of a mantelpiece. **Wallies** are false (porcelain) teeth.

wanchancy   unlucky, with supernatural undertones.
>   'And then the ae boat set aff for North Berwick, an' the tither lay whaur it was and watched the **wanchancy** thing on the brae-side.'
>   Robert Louis Stevenson, *Catriona*, 1893

warklooms   tools of a trade.
>   'I was i' the mean time delvin out the ministers butt, an brok my **wark loom**; an ga'n to seek a lean o' the beadle's, they ran in before me, an gar'd his wife cry, com in by Henry an get the fashion of the house.'
>   'Henry Blyth's Contract containing An Account of the Way and Manner of His Wooing his lass, in a fine and elegant Discourse to the Minister's Wife, his Mistress', 1800

warsle   to wrestle (with life).
>   'Effort needit tae **warsle** agin the blafferts.' ['Effort needed to walk against the wind.']
>   Chris Robinson and Eileen Finlayson, *Scottish Weather*, 2008

wash   in whisky-making, the liquid of water, fermented barley and yeast, which is then distilled. The vat or tub for this mixture is called a 'washback'.

watergaw   rainbow; see also **silk napkin**.

watt   unit of power named in honour of steam-engine inventor James Watt (1736–1819).

wauckle   stagger, possibly because of drink. See **wee Macwhackle**.

waulk   traditionally, to beat, soak and pound cloth by hand to make it heavier and denser. Today, the call-and-response songs that the women who carried out the **waulking** in the **Gaelic** areas of Scotland are all that remains of this **crofting** process.

Waverley   Edinburgh's main railway terminus; believed to be the only station in the world named after a novel.

wean [*way-n*]   child; literally, 'wee one'. 'Weans World' is a baby's and children's clothing store on Glasgow's Trongate.

webster/wabster   1. weaver; 2. spider.
'Slaughter. 23 July 1597 – Andro Rewll, **Webster** (weaver) in Corstorphin. Dilatit of **airt** and pairt of the slauchter of vmqle Johnne Rewll, his sone, ane **barne** of xii yeir auld; committit the xxi of June lastbypast.' ['Andro Rewll, weaver in Corstorphin. Accused of the murder of (deceased) Johnne Rewll, his son, a child of 12 years old; committed on 21 June last year.']
Criminal Trials in Scotland: 1596–1609

wee   small. Famous Scots of diminutive stature: wee Willie Winkie; Wee Eck in Oor Wullie; the Wee MacGregor; **wee Macwhackle**; wee Jimmy Kranky; and, of course, the **Wee Man**.

wee Macwhackle   a toddler; literally, 'little son of **wauckle**'.

wee man   literally, 'a small person'; 1. used to describe a person of small physical stature; 2. used as a greeting; 3. God; 4. the devil. That it can mean both God and the devil is very Scottish – see **antisyzygy**.

wee sma' hours   after midnight – a time you might encounter too many Scots convinced they are Frank Sinatra, crooning his 1955 album *In the Wee Small Hours*.

Weegie   Glaswegian.

weel-kent   well known, famous, usual: 'Ye ken who ah mean, thingummyjig. She's a **weel-kent** face.'

wersh   1. pale or wan; 2. queasy, feeling under the weather with no precise symptoms; see **wabbit**.

whaup   curlew (*Numenius arquata*).

whaur   where: '**Whaur**'s yir Wullie Shakespeare **noo**?' – reputedly shouted by a member of the audience overcome by patriotic euphoria at the end of the 1756 production of *The Douglas* by John Hume. More sober reflection might bring one to the conclusion that – despite being English – Mr Shakespeare is the better dramatist; hence the phrase often being used with considerable irony.

wheech   to move fast, go about things in a speedy manner, fast.

wheen   a lot or fairly big amount.
   '"Why?" asked Wat, perplexed. "What use are a **wheen** of old housewives to anybody but the **bairns** they care for? I ken they like knowing all about everything but gossip won't save the world – or save me either."'
   Alasdair Gray, *A History Maker*, 2005

wheesht   shh, quiet.
   'When the voice of man was **wheesht**, and all was sunk in the sound sleep of midnight.'
   D. M. Moir, *The Life of Mansie Wauch*, 1839

whigmaleerie   something fanciful and over-elaborate; unnecessarily decorative.

whisky, see **usquebaugh**.

white pudding, see **mealy-pudding**.

whitrick   weasel or stoat (*Mustela*); literally, 'white rat'.

Whitsun, see **quarter days**.

widdershins   anti-clockwise; considered unlucky. See also **deasil**.
   'A cat walking **widdershins** on Hallowe'en – that was a thing to
   send a shiver down the spine!'
   F. Marian McNeill, *The Silver Bough*, 1968

wilkies, see **tummel**.

Willie-whip-the-wind   kestrel (*Falco tinnunculus*).

winch   literally, 'pick up'; used to describe the mating ritual of the
Scots: 'Check them oot. Met up the dancin', **winchin'** away.'

wise   way, as in 'no wise' ('no way').

workie   ubiquitous name for a worker, usually engaged in a manual
task.
   'There once was a fat **workie**. You've seen him before. High-vis
   jacket, helmet, steel-toe capped boots. And a belly like a space
   hopper. He grafted all day, every day.'
   Limmy, *Daft Wee Stories*, 2016

worricow   a nasty hobgoblin type of supernatural harasser.

wrangeous   unjust.

> *I will not father my bairn on you,*
> *Nor on no **wrangeous** man,*
> *Though ye would give him to his dowry*
> *Five thousand ploughs of land.*

Traditional

wynd (Old Norse, *venda*)   narrow lane or passageway in a town or village.

yowe

yer/yir   1. you are; 2. your.

Yer at yir grannie's   hospitable invitation, i.e. at your grandmother's house you will not be denied anything.

yer grannie   disbelieving response to a lie. Sir Walter Scott wrote in his *Journal* in 1826, 'Dined with the Duke of Wellington . . . I wish for **sheep's head** and whisky toddy against all the French cookery and champagne in the world.' To which the response should be, '**Yer grannie!**' See also **maw**.

yowe   ewe.

yowe trummle   unseasonably cold weather in early summer to make a ewe shiver.

> 'We have still to weather the borrowing days, the caul' gab,
> the coo's quake, and the **yowe trummle** before we are clear of
> unpleasant weather.'
> *Aberdeen Press And Journal*, 8 March 1930

BIBLIOGRAPHY

Dictionary of the Scots Language/Dictionar o the Scots Leid (DSL)
Scottish Language Dictionaries is Scotland's independent lexicographical body for the Scots language, responsible for the major dictionaries of the Scots language.

More information about about its work and publications can be found at https://dsl.ac.uk.

Baxter, Stanley, *The Parliamo Glasgow Omnibus* (Birlinn, Edinburgh, 2002)

Collins English Dictionary Complete and Unabridged, 13th edn (HarperCollins, Glasgow, 2018)

Collins Gem Scottish Dictionary (HarperCollins, Glasgow, 2014)

Crofton, Ian, *A Dictionary of Scottish Phrase and Fable* (Birlinn, Edinburgh, 2016)

Donaldson, David (ed.), *A Supplement to Jamieson's Scottish Dictionary* (Alexander Gardner, Paisley, 1887)

Dwelly, Edward, *Illustrated Gaelic–English Dictionary* (Birlinn, Edinburgh, 1993)

Jamieson, J. J., *A Dictionary of the Scots Language*, abridged by John Johnstone (William Tait, Edinburgh, 1846)

MacDonald, Aeneas, *Whisky* (Canongate, Edinburgh, 2006)

MacNeill, Morag, *Everyday Gaelic* (Birlinn, Edinburgh, 2006)

Millar, Robert McColl, *Northern and Insular Scots* (EUP, Edinburgh, 2007)

Munro, Michael, *The Complete Patter* (Canongate, Edinburgh, 1999)

Shepherd, Robbie, and Norman Harper, *Dash o Doric: The Hale Lot* (Birlinn, Edinburgh, 2007)

Stott, Louis, *Scottish History in Verse* (Mainstream, Edinburgh, 2013)

Thomson, Amanda, *A Scots Dictionary of Nature* (Saraband, Glasgow, 2018)

Thomson, Derick S., *The New English–Gaelic Dictionary* (Gairm, Glasgow, 2003)

Watson, Norman, *The Dundee Dicshunury* (Dundee, 2011)

SOURCES FOR QUOTATIONS

Introduction

Robert Leighton, 'Scotch Words', Scotch Words, and The bapteesement o' the bairn (Routledge & Sons, London, 1869)

Vincent, St, of Lerins, 'Commonitorium', translated into Scots by Ninian Winzet (Antwerp, 1563)

Book of Common Order (Edinburgh, 1578)

James Johnston, Robert Burns et al., *The Scots Musical Museum* (Edinburgh, 1803)

Julia Donaldson, *The Doric Gruffalo*, illustrated by Axel Scheffler, translated into Doric by Sheena Blackhall (Itchy Coo, Edinburgh, 2016)

Julia Donaldson, *Thi Dundee Gruffalo*, illustrated by Axel Scheffler, translatit intil Dundonian beh Matthew Fitt (Itchy Coo, Edinburgh, 2016)

Julia Donaldson, *The Glasgow Gruffalo*, illustrated by Axel Scheffler, translated intae Glaswegian Scots by Elaine C. Smith (Itchy Coo, Edinburgh 2016)

Julia Donaldson, *The Orkney Gruffalo*, illustrated by Axel Scheffler, translated into Orcadian Scots by Simon W. Hall (Itchy Coo, Edinburgh, 2016)

Julia Donaldson, *The Shetland Gruffalo*, illustrated by Axel Scheffler, translated into Shetland Scots by Laureen Johnson (Itchy Coo, Edinburgh, 2016)

James Kelman, *How Late It Was, How Late* (Vintage, London, 1998)

Irvine Welsh, *Trainspotting* (Vintage, London, 1994)

Robert McColl Millar, *Northern and Insular Scots* (EUP, Edinburgh, 2007)

Dictionary

a': *The Canongate Burns: The Complete Poems and Songs of Robert Burns*, edited by Andrew Noble and Patrick Scott Hogg (Canongate, Edinburgh, 2001)

Abbot of Unreason: Sir Walter Scott, *The Abbot* (Dent, London, 1936)

a'body: *Oor Wullie Annual* (Paragon Books, Bath, 2017)

abune: in Andrew O'Hagan (ed.), *A Night Out with Robert Burns* (Canongate, Edinburgh, 2008)

agley: *The Canongate Burns: The Complete Poems and Songs of Robert Burns*, edited by Andrew Noble and Patrick Scott Hogg (Canongate, Edinburgh, 2001)

ahent/ahint: Violet Jacob, *Songs of Angus* (John Murray, London, 1915)

aiblins: *John Buchan's Collected Poems*, edited by Andrew Lownie and William Milne (Scottish Cultural Press, Newbattle, 1986)

antisyzygy: C. Gregory Smith, *Scottish Literature: Character and Influence* (1919), referenced in *Dictionary of the Scots Language* (*DSL*), Scottish Language Dictionaries, dsl.ac.uk.

antrin: Lewis Grassic Gibbon, *Grey Granite*, the final novel of the trilogy *Scots Quair* (Polygon, Edinburgh, 2006)

athegither: Bram Stoker, *Dracula* (Arrow, London, 1980)

ay: Sir David Lyndsay of the Mount, 'The Answer Quhilk Schir David Lindesay Maid to the Kingis Flyting', in Sir David Lyndsay, *Six Scottish Courtly and Chivalric Poems, Including Lyndsay's 'Squyer Meldrum'*, edited by Rhiannon Purdie and Emily Wingfield (Medieval Institute Publishing, Kalamazoo, Michigan, 2018)

bagpipes: *The Complaynte of Scotland* (Scottish Text Society, Edinburgh, 1979)

baillie: Sir Walter Scott, *Rob Roy* (Penguin, Harmondsworth, 1995)

barley-bree: Song submitted to *Edinburgh Literary Journal*, signed 'W. W.', 1830

bawer: Robert Henryson, 'Testament of Cresseid', fifteenth century

belly-huddroun: William Dunbar, 'The Dance of the Sevin Deidly Synnis', in John and Winifred MacQueen (eds), *A Choice of Scottish Verse 1470–1570* (Faber & Faber, London, 1972)

blast: 'The First Blast of the Trumpet Against the Monstrous Regiment of Women', published by John Knox in 1558; 'Oh wert thou in the cauld blast', in *The Canongate Burns: The Complete Poems and Songs of Robert Burns* (Canongate Classics, Edinburgh, 2001)

bleezin': Sir Walter Scott, *Rob Roy* (Penguin, Harmondsworth, 1995)

bluebell: *The Scots Musical Museum*, 1803

boak: Liz Lochhead, *Tartuffe* (after Molière), in *Misery Guts and Tartuffe* (Nick Hern Books, London, 2002)

bogey: James Kelman, *A Chancer* (Picador, London, 1987)

bogie: Harry Lauder, 'Roamin' in the Gloamin'' (1911)

bonnet laird: Robert Louis Stevenson, *Weir of Hermiston* (Chatto & Windus, London, 1913)

bonnie: Harry Lauder, 'I Love a Lassie' (1907)

bonnie-penny: Nan Shepherd, *Quarry Wood* (Canongate, Edinburgh, 2018)

Border, the: Sir Walter Scott, 'Blue Bonnets Over the Border', in *Illustrated Book of Scottish Songs* (Nathaniel Cooke, London, 1854)

breenge: Stuart A. Paterson, 'Breenge', in *Aye* (Tapsalteerie Press, Tarland, Aberdeenshire, 2016)

bumfle: Kimberley Freeman, *Evergreen Falls* (Touchstone, New York, 2015)

bunnet: John Reston, 'In Memory of Keir Hardie Entering the House of Commons', in Ian Crofton (ed.), *A Dictionary of Scottish Phrase and Fable* (Birlinn, Edinburgh, 2016)

Burns Night: Robert Burns, letter to W. Simpson, May 1785

Burns Supper: Robert Burns, 'Address to the Haggis', in Andrew O'Hagan, *A Night Out with Robert Burns* (Canongate, Edinburgh, 2008)

byke: letter of 26 July 1852 in Clyde De L. Ryals, et al. (eds), *The Collected Letters of Thomas and Jane Welsh Carlyle*, vol. 27 (Duke University Press, Durham, North Carolina, 1999)

cabbieclaw: Annette Hope, *A Caledonian Feast* (Canongate, Edinburgh, 2002)

Caledonia: Tacitus, *Agricola* (Penguin, Harmondsworth, 1964)

camstairy or camsteerie: Edwin Morgan, *The Whittrick: A Poem in Eight Dialogues* (Akros, Kirkcaldy, 1973)

cantrip: Robert Burns, 'Tam o'Shanter – a tale', in Andrew O'Hagan, *A Night Out with Robert Burns* (Canongate, Edinburgh, 2008)

cateran: Sir Walter Scott, *Waverley* (Archibald Constable & Co., Edinburgh, 1814)

causey: John Galt, *The Provost* (OUP, Oxford, 1982)

chief: James Macpherson, *The Poems of Ossian* (Boston, 1857)

clanjamfrie: David Greig, *Pyrenees*, in *Selected Plays 1999–2009* (Faber & Faber, London, 2010)

cleg: Agnes Owens, *Like Birds in the Wilderness* (HarperCollins, London, 1987)

clipe: *The Scottish Education Journal*, Vol. 27, 1944

clockwork orange, the: Douglas Corrance and Ian Archer, *Glasgow from the Eye in the Sky* (Mainstream Publishing, Edinburgh, 1988)

cludgie: Glenn Chandler, *Taggart's Glasgow* (Lennard, Glasgow, 1989)

collops: F. Marian McNeill, *The Scots Kitchen: Its Lore and Recipes* (Birlinn, Edinburgh, 2010)

coronach: Alexander Carmichael, *Carmina Gadelica* (Floris Books, Edinburgh, 1992)

corrieneuchin': Norman MacCaig, 'Two Thoughts of MacDiarmid in a quiet place', in Ewen MacCaig (ed.), *The Poems of Norman MacCaig* (Birlinn, Edinburgh, 2009)

coupon: Jeff Torrington, *Swing Hammer Swing!* (Vintage, London, 1992)

crabbit: William Dunbar, 'The Golden Targe', in *A Book of Scottish Verse*, selected by R. L. Mackie (Oxford University Press, London, 1968)

cutty: Robert Burns, 'Tam o'Shanter – a tale', in Andrew O'Hagan, *A Night Out with Robert Burns* (Canongate, Edinburgh, 2008)

daft days: Neil Munro, *The Daft Days* (Blackwood, Edinburgh, 1907)

deasil: Thomas Pennant, *A Tour in Scotland, 1769* (Birlinn, Edinburgh, 2019)

deil: Robert Henryson, 'Moral Fables', in John and Winifred MacQueen (eds), *A Choice of Scottish Verse 1470–1570*, (Faber & Faber, London, 1972)

dicht: Robert Henryson, 'The Bludy Serk', *c.* 1500

dirl: George Douglas Brown, *The House with the Green Shutters* (Penguin, Harmondsworth, 1985)

dog: Alison Irvine, *This Road is Red* (Luath, Edinburgh, 2011)

dominie: J. M. Barrie, 'Auld Licht Idylls', in *The Novels, Tales and Sketches of J. M. Barrie* (Scrivener, New York, 1927)

doo: George MacDonald, *David Elginbrod* (Hurst and Blackett, London, 1863)

Doric: George Malcolm Thomson, *The Rediscovery of Scotland* (Kegan Paul, Trench, Trübner & Co., London, 1928)

draunting: Allan Ramsay, *A Collection of Scots Proverbs* (Oliver & Boyd, Edinburgh, nineteenth century)

dree one's weird: James Hogg, *Collected Novels, Scottish Mystery Tales and Fantasy Stories*, e-artnow.org, 2017

drookit: J. J. Bell, *The Wee Macgreegor* (Ogilvie, Glasgow, 1903)

drooth/drouth: Robert Burns, 'Tam o'Shanter – a tale', in Andrew O'Hagan, *A Night Out with Robert Burns* (Canongate, Edinburgh, 2008)

eident: John Gibson Lockhart, *Memoirs of the Life of Sir Walter Scott*, vol. 4 (Cambridge University Press, 2013)

elfhame: Dane Love, *Legendary Ayrshire: Custom, Folklore, Tradition* (Carn Publishing, Ayr, 2009)

ettle: Naomi Mitchison, *Bull Calves* (Virago, London, 1997)

fanny: Irvine Welsh, *A Decent Ride* (Jonathan Cape, London, 2015)

ferlie: Mollie Hunter, *The Ferlie* (Blackie & Son, Glasgow, 1968)

feu: Benjamin Disraeli, *Henrietta Temple: A Love Story* (Baudry, Paris, 1837)

fey: Monica Germanà, *Scottish Women's Gothic and Fantastic Writing* (Edinburgh University Press, 2010)

fiere: Robert Burns, 'For Auld Lang Syne', in G .F. Maine (ed.), *The Songs of Robert Burns* (Collins, London and Glasgow, 2016)

fiery cross: General Wade, quoted in David Brewster, *The Edinburgh Encyclopaedia* (Blackwood, Edinburgh, 1830)

filibeg/philibeg: Robert Louis Stevenson, *Kidnapped* (Puffin, Harmondsworth, 1995)

fitba: W. A. Craigie (ed.), *The Maitland Folio Manuscript, containing poems by Sir Richard Maitland, Dunbar, Douglas, Henryson, and others* (Edinburgh, 1913–27), referenced in *DSL*; Hugh McIlvanney, *McIlvanney on Football* (Mainstream, Edinburgh, 1999)

fleein': Edward Bannerman Ramsay, Dean of Edinburgh, *Reminiscences of Scottish Life and Character* (Gall & Inglis, London, 1875)

flit: William Cobbett, *The Life of Thomas Paine* (New York, G. P. Putnam, 1892)

flype: Alexander Montgomerie, 'The Flyting betwixt Montgomerie and Polwart', *c.* 1585

forby: Martin Luther, *Writings*, referenced in *DSL*; J. M. Barrie, *A Window in Thrums* (Saltire Society, Edinburgh, 2003)

forefochen: William Craig Brownlee, *A Careful and Free Inquiry Into the True Nature and Tendency of the Society of Friends*, 1824

fou: Robert Burns, 'Tam o'Shanter – a tale', in Andrew O'Hagan, *A Night Out with Robert Burns* (Canongate, Edinburgh, 2008)

fykie: ibid.

fyre-flaught: John Lamont, *The Diary of Mr John Lamont of Newton. 1649–1671* (Edinburgh, 1830)

gadgie: Tim Neat, *Hamish Henderson: The Making of the Poet* (Birlinn, Edinburgh, 2012)

gangrel: George P. Dunbar, *A Whiff o' the Doric* (D. Wyllie & Son, Aberdeen, 1922)

gauger: Norman MacCaig, 'A Man in Assynt', in Ewen MacCaig (ed.), *The Poems of Norman MacCaig* (Birlinn, Edinburgh, 2009)

Gay Gordons: Henry Newbolt, 'The Gay Gordons' (1897)

glamour/glamer/glawmir: *Satirical Poems of the Time of the Reformation* (Scottish Text Society, Edinburgh, 1891)

gloamin': Harry Lauder, 'Roamin' in the Gloamin'' (1911)

gowan: Alexander Montgomerie, 'The Night is Neir Gone', sixteenth century

gowk: William Soutar, 'The Gowk', in Carl MacDougall and Douglas Gifford (eds), *Into a Room: Selected Poems of William Soutar* (Argyll Publishing, Glendaruel, 2000)

gralloch: John Buchan, *John Macnab* (Birlinn, Edinburgh, 2007)

greet: Robert Coltart, 'Coulter's Candy', *c.* 1845

gumption: epistle from William Hamilton to Allan Ramsay, 24 July 1719, in James Grant Wilson (ed.), *The Poets and Poetry of Scotland: From the Earliest to the Present . . .*, vol. 1 (Harper, New York, 1876)

haar: Sheena Blackhall, 'November: A Scots owersett o a Poem bi John Clare', in *Tick-Tock: Poems in Scots & English* (Lochlands, Maud, 2010)

hackit: Roald Dahl, *Matilda in Scots*, translated by Anne Donovan (Itchy Coo, Edinburgh, 2019)

haver: Sir Walter Scott, *Redgauntlet*, 1824

hem/hames/haimes and brechom: Allan Ramsay, *Tea Time Miscellany* (London, 1733)

Highland fling: Grant F. Scott (ed.), *Selected Letters of John Keats* (Harvard University Press, Cambridge, Massachusetts, 2005)

hippit: Jessie Kesson, *The White Bird Passes* (Black & White, Edinburgh, 2017)

hirple: Allan Boyd, *The Prophecies of Thomas Rymer . . . Carefully collected and compared with ancient old prophecies and the book of arias* (Glasgow, 1826)

hoatchin': Ian Rankin, *Black and Blue* (Orion, London, 1997)

honest men and bonie lasses: Robert Burns, 'Tam o'Shanter – a tale', in Andrew O'Hagan, *A Night Out with Robert Burns* (Canongate, Edinburgh, 2008)

hoot: F. A. Pottle (ed.), *Boswell and the Grand Tour: Germany and Switzerland 1764* (William Heinemann, London, 1953)

houghmagandie: Robert Burns, *The Merry Muses of Caledonia* (Luath, Edinburgh, 2009)

hurdies: Sir David Lindsay, *Ane Satyre of the Thrie Estaitis* (Canongate, Edinburgh, 2012)

ilka: Jean Elliot, 'The Flowers of the Forest', in *A Book of Scottish Verse*, selected by R. L. Mackie (Oxford University Press, London, 1968)

imphm: George Douglas Brown, *The House with the Green Shutters* (Penguin, Harmondsworth, 1985)

ither: Robert Burns, 'To a Louse (On Seeing One on a Lady's Bonnet, at Church)', in *Poems, Chiefly in the Scottish Dialect* (Luath, Edinburgh, 2009)

jalouse: Billy Kay, *The Scottish World: A Journey into the Scottish Diaspora* (Mainstream, Edinburgh, 2008)

jeely: Robert Louis Stevenson, *Weir of Hermiston* (Chatto & Windus, London, 1913)

jobby: Billy Connolly, *Classic Connolly* (remastered CD), (Spectrum Audio, 2008)

kiggle-kaggle: J. G. Grant, *The Complete Curler* (1914), referenced in *DSL*

lament: William Dunbar, 'Lament for the Makaris', in John and Winifred MacQueen (eds), *A Choice of Scottish Verse 1470–1570* (Faber & Faber, London, 1972)

land of the mountain and the flood: Sir Walter Scott, *Lay of the Last Minstrel, A Poem* (Birlinn, Edinburgh, 2013)

lassie: Anna Durand, *Gift-Wrapped in a Kilt* (Jacobsville Books, Lake Linden, Michigan, 2018)

leal/leyil: C. Innes (ed.), *The Book of the Thanes of Cawdor; a Series of Papers selected from the Charter Room at Cawdor, 1236–1742* (Spalding Club, Aberdeen, 1859), referenced in *DSL*.

lea-rig: Robert Fergusson, 'The Lee Rig', in James Gray (ed.), *The Poems of Robert Fergusson* (Oliver & Boyd, Macredie & Co., Edinburgh, 1821)

lift: Hector Boece, *The History and Chronicles of Scotland*, written in Latin and translated by John Bellenden, Archdeacon of Moray (W. & C. Tait, Edinburgh, 1821), referenced in *DSL*.

lockfast: *The Exchequer Rolls of Scotland, 1264–1600* (General Register House, Edinburgh, 1878–1908), referenced in *DSL*.

machair: 'Michael the Victorious', in Alexander Carmichael, *Carmina Gadelica* (Floris Books, Edinburgh, 1992)

mankit: Graham Chapman, Terry Gilliam, Michael Palin, et al., *Monty Python and the Holy Grail: Monty Python's Flying Circus: Just the Words*, vols 1 and 2 (Mandarin, London, 1990)

Master: Robert Louis Stevenson, *The Master of Ballantrae and Weir of Hermiston* (Birlinn, Edinburgh, 2008)

meevin': Jock Duncan, *Jock's Jocks: Voices of Scottish Soldiers from the First World War*, edited by Gary West (NMS, Edinburgh, 2019)

midge: Neil Munro, *Para Handy* (Birlinn, Edinburgh, 2002)

Mons Meg: H. J. C. Grierson (ed.), *The Letters of Sir Walter Scott: 1828–1831* (Constable, London, 1932)

nip a dram: Agnes Owens, *Agnes Owens: The Complete Short Stories* (Edinburgh, Birlinn, 2011)

nuttata: Norman Watson, *The Dundee Dicshunury* (Dundee, 2011)

ochone: Marion Campbell, Mrs MacGregor of Glenstrae, 'Griogal Cridhe/ Lament for MacGregor of Glenstrae', in Robert Crawford and Mick Imlah (eds), *The Penguin Book of Scottish Verse* (Penguin, Harmondsworth, 2006); Robert Henryson, 'Testament of Cresseid', in John and Winifred MacQueen (eds), *A Choice of Scottish Verse 1470–1570* (Faber & Faber, London, 1972)

ocht: Blind Harry, *The Wallace* (Ogle & Co., Glasgow, 1869)

outwith: Scottish Parliament: Act anent the Mynes, 1593, quoted in Robert William Cochran-Patrick, *Early Records Relating to Mining in Scotland* (David Douglas, Edinburgh, 1878)

owergyaan: *The Complaynt of Scotland*, in James Henry Dixon (ed.), *Scottish Traditional Versions of Ancient Ballads*, vol. 17 (The Percy Society, London, 1845)

panel: Alasdair Alpin MacGregor, *The Golden Lamp* (Michael Joseph, London, 1964)

pawky: John Galt, *The Provost* (OUP, Oxford, 1982)

peel: David MacGibbon and Thomas Ross, *The Castellated and Domestic Architecture of Scotland from the Twelfth to the Eighteenth Century*, vol. 5 (D. Douglas, Edinburgh, 1892)

peenie: Nan Shepherd, *The Weatherhouse* (Canongate, Edinburgh, 2016)

pee-the-bed: Sally Magnusson, *The Life of Pee* (Aurum Press, London, 2010)

peh: David Phillips, 'Pehs' (1966), in Norman Watson, *The Dundee Dicshunury* (Dundee, 2011)

pibroch: Mairi Nighean Alasdair Ruiadh/Mary McLeod, 'Tuireadh'/'Blue Song', English version by Robert Crawford, in Robert Crawford and Mick Imlah (eds), *The Penguin Book of Scottish Verse* (Penguin, Harmondsworth, 2006)

Pict: 'The Miracles of St Nynia', Thomas Owen Clancy (ed.), *The Triumph Tree* (Canongate, Edinburgh, 1998)

pintil: *Fergusson's Scottish Proverbs*, 1641

pit awa': Ellen Johnston, 'The Last Sark', in Robert Crawford and Mick Imlah (eds), *The Penguin Book of Scottish Verse* (Penguin, Harmondsworth, 2006)

pot still: Rachel McCormack, *Chasing the Dram: Finding the Spirit of Whisky* (Simon & Schuster, London, 2017)

potted-heid: Margaret Bennett, *Oatmeal and the Catechism: Scottish Gaelic Settlers in Quebec* (John Donald, Edinburgh & Eastern Townships, Quebec, 2003)

puddock: John M. Caie, 'The Puddock', in *The Kindly North: Verse in Scots and English* (D. Wyllie & Son, Aberdeen, 1934)

quean/quine: Records of the Kirk Session of Brechin MS vol. I (1615–77), referenced in *DSL*.

quhat: James Craigie (ed.), *The Poems of King James VI of Scotland*, 2 vols. (Scottish Text Society, Edinburgh, 1955, 1958)

quhen: 'Makbeth' in David Laing (ed.), *The Orygynal Cronykil of Scotland by Andrew of Wyntoun*, vol. 2 (Edinburgh, 1872)

quhilk: Mary, Queen of Scots, 'Sonnet to Bothwell', anonymous translation from the original Latin in Robert Crawford and Mick Imlah (eds), *The Penguin Book of Scottish Verse* (Penguin, Harmondsworth, 2006)

rumgumption: James Beattie, 'To Mr Alexander Ross', in John Ross (ed.), *The Book of Scottish Poems: Ancient and Modern* (Edinburgh, 1878)

scart: John Beaton, in *The Scottish Naturalist* (Oliver & Boyd, Edinburgh, 1924)

Scottishness: Irvine Welsh, *Trainspotting* (Vintage, London, 1994)

scrieve: Rab Wilson, 'Ye need a gey thick skin tae scrieve in Scots!', in *The National* newspaper, 12 April 2018

scunner: *The Scotch Haggis: a miscellaneous compilation, illustrative of Scottish wit* (Duncan Campbell & Co., Glasgow, 1875)

semmit: *Review of Scottish Culture*, issue 20 (John Donald Publishers and National Museum of Antiquities of Scotland, Edinburgh, 2008)

shanky/shunkey: Robin Jenkins, *Just Duffy* (Canongate, Edinburgh, 1988)

shairn/sharn: Samuel Hibbert, *A Description of the Shetland Isles* (T. & J. Manson, Lerwick, 1931)

sheep's heid: Robert Semple of Beltrees, 'The Wedding of Maggie and Jock', *c.* 1650; referenced in *DSL*.

sherrackin': Alexander McArthur and Herbert Kingsley Long, *No Mean City* (Corgi, London, 1978)

silver darlings: Neil Gunn, *The Silver Darlings* (Faber & Faber, London, 1978)

slaister: Nigel Tranter, *The Story of Scotland* (Neil Wilson Publishing, Glasgow, 1987)

sleekit: Robert Burns, 'To a Mouse', in Andrew O'Hagan, *A Night Out with Robert Burns* (Canongate, Edinburgh, 2008)

slogan: Sir George Mackenzie of Rosehaugh, *The science of herauldry treated as part of the civil law and law of nations, etc.* (Edinburgh, 1680); referenced in *DSL*.

smeddum: Lewis Grassic Gibbon, *Smeddum* (Canongate Books, Edinburgh, 2001), and *Cloud Howe*, in *A Scots Quair* (Penguin, Harmondsworth, 1990)

smirr: Neil Munro, *John Splendid* (William Blackwood and Sons, Edinburgh, 1898)

smit/smote: John Knox, *Selected Writings* (Committee of the General Assembly of the Free Church of Scotland for the Publication of the Works of Scottish Reformers and Divines, Edinburgh, 1845); referenced in *DSL*.

smoor: Alexander Carmichael, 'Smooring Blessing', in *Carmina Gadelica* (Floris Books, Edinburgh, 1992)

sna' aff a dyke: John Galt, *Annals of the Parish* (OUP, Oxford, 1986)

sonsie/sonsy: Tobias Smollett, *The Reprisal, or The Tars of Old England: A Comedy*, 1757

souch/sough: Gavin Douglas, *The Aeneid* in John Small (ed.), *The Poetical Works of Gavin Douglas, Bishop of Dunkeld*, vol. 4 (William Paterson, Edinburgh, 1874)

soutar/souter: Robert Burns, 'Tam o'Shanter – a tale', in Andrew O'Hagan, *A Night Out with Robert Burns* (Canongate, Edinburgh, 2008)

speir: J. Derrick McClure, *Doric: The Dialect of North-East Scotland* (John Benjamins Publishing Company, Amsterdam, Netherlands, 2002)

Stone of Scone: Johnny McEvoy, 'The Wee Magic Stane', on Sangstories the Sangschule of Linlithgow website, copyright © 2012

sugarallie: J. M. Barrie, *A Window in Thrums* (Saltire Society, Edinburgh, 2003)

syne: Robert Burns, 'For Auld Lang Syne', in G .F. Maine (ed.), *The Songs of Robert Burns* (Collins, London and Glasgow, 2016)

tatterdemalion: quoted in Ian Crofton, *A Dictionary of Scottish Phrase and Fable* (Birlinn, Edinburgh, 2016)

thirl: John Barbour (ed.), *The Buik of the Most Noble and Valiant Conqueror Alexander the Grit* (C. W. Blackwood & Son, London, 1929)

thrang: Robert Fergusson, 'Leith Races', in James Gray (ed.), *The Poems of Robert Fergusson* (Oliver & Boyd, Macredie & Co., Edinburgh, 1821)

thrapple: James Hogg, 'The Village of Balmaquhapple', in *The Poetical Works of the Etterick Shepherd*, vol. 5 (Blackie & Son, Glasgow, 1839)

tousie: Robert Burns, 'The Twa Dogs', *Poems, Chiefly in the Scottish Dialect* (Luath, Edinburgh, 2009)

tup: Dorothy Dunnett, *Checkmate* (Penguin, Harmondsworth, 1999)

tweed: Finlay J. MacDonald, *Crowdie and Cream* (Sphere, London, 1995)

two New Years: Neil Munro, *Para Handy* (Birlinn, Edinburgh, 2002)

Union, the: Christopher A. Whatley, *Scots and the Union: Then and Now* (Edinburgh University Press, 2014)

upsitten: Patrick Walker, *The Life of Peden*; quoted in *DSL*.

usquebaugh/uisge beatha: Compton Mackenzie, *The Highland Omnibus: Monarch of the Glen, Whisky Galore and Rival Monster* (Penguin, Harmondsworth, 1983)

vaunty: Joanna Baillie, 'Fy let us a' to the Wedding', in Judith Bailey Slagle (ed.), *Collected Letters of Joanna Baillie*, vol. 1 (Fairleigh Dickinson University Press, Madison, New Jersey, 1999)

visek: George Low, *A Tour through the Islands of Orkney and Shetland* (W. Peace, Orkney, 1879)

vogie: James Hogg, *The Jacobite Relics of Scotland: being the songs, airs and legends of the adherents of the House of Stuart* (Edinburgh University Press, 2002)

wanchancy: Robert Louis Stevenson, *Catriona*, in *The Scottish Novels* (Canongate, Edinburgh, 1997)

warklooms: 'Henry Blyth's Contract containing An Account of the Way and Manner of His Wooing his lass, in a fine and elegant Discourse to the Minister's Wife, his Mistress', chapbook printed and sold by John Morren, Earl Campbell's Close, Cowgate, Edinburgh, 1800, in the collection of the National Library of Scotland, Edinburgh

warsle: Chris Robinson and Eileen Finlayson, *Scottish Weather* (Black & White, Edinburgh, 2008)

webster: Robert Pitcairn, *Criminal Trials in Scotland: 1596–1609* (William Tait, Edinburgh, 1833)

wheen: Alasdair Gray, *A History Maker* (Canongate, Edinburgh, 2005)

wheesht: D. M. Moir, *The Life of Mansie Wauch* (William Blackwood and Sons, Edinburgh, 1839)

widdershins: F. Marian McNeill, *The Silver Bough* (Canongate, Edinburgh, 2001)

workie: Limmy, *Daft Wee Stories* (Arrow, London, 2016)

wrangeous: Francis J. Child (ed.), *English and Scottish Popular Ballads* (Dover, New York, 2003)

yer grannie: Sir Walter Scott, *Journal*, 15 November 1826 (Burt Franklin, New York, 1890)

yowe trummle: *Aberdeen Press And Journal*, 8 March 1930, in DSL (https://www.dsl.ac.uk/entry/snd/yowe)

ABOUT THE AUTHOR

Born in Glasgow, writer and bookseller **Robin A. Crawford** has a particular interest in the culture and natural heritage of his native land. He is the critically acclaimed author of *Into The Peatlands: A Journey Through the Moorland Year*, longlisted for the Highland Book Prize 2019. He lives in Fife, Scotland, with his wife.